AA

# Italian

## phrase book

AA Publishing

# Contents

English edition prepared by First Edition Translations Ltd, Great Britain

Designed and produced by AA Publishing

First published in 1995 as Wat & Hoe Italiaans, © Uitgeverij Kosmos bv - Utrecht/Antwerpen
Van Dale Lexicografie bv - Utrecht/Antwerpen


Reprinted 1997, Jun and Sep 1998, Oct 1999, Feb and Sep 2000
Reprinted Apr and Sep 2001, May and Dec 2002
Reprinted Dec 2003. Reprinted May, Aug and Dec 2004
Reprinted Apr 2005
Reprinted Apr and Aug 2006
Reprinted Feb and May 2007



A CIP catalogue record for this book is available from the British Library

Published by AA Publishing (a trading name of Automobile Association Developments Limited, whose registered office is Fanum House, Basing View, Basingstoke, Hampshire RG21 4EA. Registered number 1878835).

A03373

Typeset by Anton Graphics Ltd, Andover, Hampshire

Printed and bound in Italy by Printer Trento S.r.l.

Find out more about AA Publishing and the wide range of services the AA provides by visiting our website at www.theAA.com/travel

# Introduction

● **Welcome to the AA's Italian Phrasebook, which contains everything you'd expect from a comprehensive language guide. It's concise, accessible and easy to understand, and you'll find it indispensable on your trip abroad.**

The guide is divided into 15 themed sections and starts with a pronunciation table which gives you the phonetic spelling to all the words and phrases you'll need to know for your trip, while at the back of the book is an extensive word list and grammar guide which will help you construct basic sentences in Italian.

Throughout the book you'll come across coloured boxes with a symbol beside them. These are designed to help you if you can't understand what your listener is saying to you. Hand the book over to them and encourage them to point to the appropriate answer to the question you are asking.

Other coloured boxes in the book – this time without the symbol – give alphabetical listings of themed words with their English translations below.

For extra clarity, we have put all English words and phrases in black, foreign language terms in red and their phonetic pronunciation in italic.

This phrasebook covers all subjects you are likely to come across during the course of your visit, from reserving a room for the night to ordering food and drink at a restaurant and what to do if your car breaks down or you lose your traveller's cheques and money. With over 2,000 commonly used words and essential phrases at your fingertips you can rest assured that you will be able to get by in all situations, so let the AA's Italian Phrasebook become your passport to a secure and enjoyable trip!

# Pronunciation table

The imitated pronunciation should be read as if it were English, bearing in mind the following main points:

## Consonants

| | | | | |
|---|---|---|---|---|
| **b, d, f, l, m, n, p, q, t, vk, j, w** | as in English<br>rarely appear in Italian | | | |
| **c** | • before **e** and **i**, like **ch** in **ch**ip | ***ch*** | cinema | ***chee**naymah* |
| | • elsewhere, like **c** in **c**at | ***k*** | casa | ***ka**hzah* |
| **ch** | like **c** in **c**at | ***k*** | chi | ***kee*** |
| **g** | • before **e** and **i**, like **j** in **j**et | ***j*** | giro | ***jee**ro* |
| | • elsewere, like **g** in **g**o | ***g*** | gatto | ***gah**tto* |
| **gh** | like **g** in **g**o | ***gh*** | funghi | *foon**ghee*** |
| **gl** | • like **lli** in mi**lli**on | ***lly*** | figlio | *fee**lly**o* |
| | • (rarely) like **gl** in En**gl**ish | ***gl*** | inglese | *een**glay**say* |
| **gn** | like **ni** in o**ni**on | ***n*** | bagno | *bah**nee**o* |
| **h** | always silent | | ho | ***o*** |
| **r** | trilled like Scottish **r** | ***r*** | riso | ***ree**zo* |
| **s** | • generally like **s** in **s**it | ***s*** | sette | ***say**ttay* |
| | • sometimes like **z** in **z**oo | ***z*** | rosa | *ro**zah*** |
| **sc** | • before e and i, like **sh** in **sh**ot | ***sh*** | pesce | *pay**shay*** |
| | • elsewhere, like **sk** in **sk**ip | ***sk*** | fresco | *fray**sko*** |
| **z,zz** | • generally like **ts** in bi**ts** | ***ts*** | grazie | *grahts**eeay*** |
| | • sometimes like **ds** in moo**ds** | ***dz*** | zero | ***dzay**ro* |

## Vowels

| | | | | |
|---|---|---|---|---|
| **a** | like **a** in c**a**r | ***ah*** | **pasta** | ***pah**stah* |
| **e** | like **ay** in w**ay** | ***ay*** | **sera** | ***say**rah* |
| **i** | like **ee** in m**ee**t | ***ee*** | **vini** | ***vee**nee* |
| **o** | like **o** in n**o**t | ***o*** | **notte** | ***no**ttay* |
| **u** | like **oo** in f**oo**t | ***oo*** | **uno** | ***oo**no* |

**Stressing of words**

Stress tends to be on the last syllable but one, e.g. fratello = frah**tay**llo; ragazza = rah**gah**tzah; italiano = eetahlee**ah**no. A number of words have a written accent on the last syllable, to indicate that the final vowel is stressed, e.g. città = cheet**tah**; caffè = kahf**fay**; lunedì = loonay**dee**.

# Useful lists

# Useful lists

Useful lists

## 1.1 Today or tomorrow?

| | |
|---|---|
| What day is it today? | Oggi, che giorno è?<br>*Odjee kay jorno ay?* |
| Today's Monday | Oggi è lunedì<br>*Odjee ay loonaydee* |
| – Tuesday | Oggi è martedì<br>*Odjee ay mahrtaydee* |
| – Wednesday | Oggi è mercoledì<br>*Odjee ay mahrkolaydee* |
| – Thursday | Oggi è giovedì<br>*Odjee ay jovaydee* |
| – Friday | Oggi è venerdì<br>*Odjee ay vaynahrdee* |
| – Saturday | Oggi è sabato<br>*Odjee ay sahbahto* |
| – Sunday | Oggi è domenica<br>*Odjee ay domayneekah* |
| in January | in gennaio<br>*een jaynnaheeo* |
| since February | da febbraio<br>*dah faybbraheeo* |
| in spring | in primavera<br>*een preemahvayrah* |
| in summer | in estate/d'estate<br>*een aystahtay* |
| in autumn | in aùtunno<br>*een ahootoonno* |
| in winter | in inverno/d'inverno<br>*een eenvayrno/deenvayrno* |
| 1997 | millenovecentonovantasette<br>*meellay/novaychaynto/novahntasayttay* |
| the twentieth century | il novecento<br>*eel novaychaynto* |
| What's the date today? | Quanti ne abbiamo oggi?<br>*Kwahntee nay abbeeahmo odjee?* |
| Today's the 24th | Oggi è il ventiquattro<br>*Odjee ay eel vaynteekwahttro* |
| Monday 3 November 1998 | lunedì, tre novembre millenovecentonovantotto<br>*loonaydee, tray novaymbray meellay/novaychaynto/novahntotto* |
| in the morning | la mattina<br>*lah mahtteenah* |
| in the afternoon | il pomeriggio<br>*eel pomayreedjo* |
| in the evening | la sera<br>*lah sayrah* |
| at night | la notte<br>*lah nottay* |
| this morning | stamattina<br>*stahmahtteenah* |

| | |
|---|---|
| this afternoon | oggi pomeriggio<br>*odjee pomayreedjo* |
| this evening | stasera<br>*stahsayhrah* |
| tonight | stanotte<br>*stahnottay* |
| last night | la notte scorsa<br>*lah nottay skorsah* |
| this week | questa settimana<br>*kwaystah saytteemahnah* |
| next month | il mese prossimo<br>*eel maysay prosseemo* |
| last year | l'anno scorso<br>*lahnno skorso* |
| next... | ...prossimo/prossima<br>*... prosseemo/prosseemah* |
| in...days/weeks/ months/years | fra...giorni/settimane/mesi/anni<br>*frah... jornee/saytteemahnay/mayzee/ahnnee* |
| ...weeks ago | ...settimane fa<br>*...saytteemahnay fah* |
| day off | giorno libero<br>*jorno leebayro* |

## 1.2 Bank holidays

● **The most important** Bank holidays in Italy are the following:

| | | |
|---|---|---|
| January 1 | New Year's Day | Capodanno |
| January 6 | Epiphany | Epifania |
| March/April | Easter and Easter Monday | Pasqua/Lunedì dell'Angelo |
| 25 April | Liberation Day | Anniversario della Liberazione (1945) |
| 1 May | Labour Day | Festa del lavoro |
| 15 August | Feast of the Assumption | Assunzione (Ferragosto) |
| 1 November | All Saints' Day | Ognissanti |
| 8 December | Feast of the Immaculate Conception | Immacolata Concezione |
| 25 December | Christmas Day | Natale |
| 26 December | Feast of Santo Stefano | Santo Stefano |

Most shops, banks and government institutions are closed on these days. Individual towns also have public holidays to celebrate their own patron saints.

## 1.3 What time is it?

| | |
|---|---|
| What time is it? | Che ore sono?<br>*Kay oray sono?* |
| It's nine o'clock | Sono le nove<br>*Sono lay novay* |
| – five past ten | Sono le dieci e cinque<br>*Sono lay deeaychy ay cheenkway* |
| – a quarter past eleven | Sono le undici e un quarto<br>*Sono lay oondeechee ay oon kwahrto* |
| – twenty past twelve | E' mezzogiorno e venti<br>*Ay maydzojorno ay vayntee* |

| | |
|---|---|
| – half past one | E' l'una e mezza<br>*Ay loonah ay maydzah* |
| – twenty–five to three | Sono le due e trentacinque<br>*Sono lay dooay ay trayntahcheenkway* |
| – a quarter to four | Sono le quattro meno un quarto<br>*Sono lay kwahttro mayno oon kwahrto* |
| – ten to five | Sono le cinque meno dieci<br>*Sono lay cheenkway mayno deeaychee* |
| It's midday (twelve noon) | E' mezzogiorno<br>*Ay maydzojorno* |
| It's midnight | E' mezzanotte<br>*Ay maydzahnottay* |
| half an hour | una mezz'ora<br>*oonah maydzorah* |
| What time? | A che ora?<br>*Ah kay orah?* |
| What time can I come round? | A che ora potrei venire?<br>*Ah kay orah potraèe vayneeray?* |
| At... | Alle...<br>*Ahllay...* |
| After... | Dopo le...<br>*Dopo lay...* |
| Before... | Prima delle...<br>*Preemah dayllay...* |
| Between...and...(o'clock) | Fra le...e le...<br>*Frah lay...ay lay...* |
| From...to... | Dalle...alle...<br>*Dahllay...ahllay...* |
| In...minutes | Fra...minuti<br>*Frah...meenootee* |
| – an hour | Fra...un'ora<br>*Frah...oonorah* |
| –...hours | Fra...ore<br>*Frah...oray* |
| – a quarter of an hour | Fra un quarto d'ora<br>*Frah oon kwahrto dorah* |
| – three quarters of an hour | Fra tre quarti d'ora<br>*Frah tray kwahrtèe dorah* |
| too early/late | troppo presto/tardi<br>*troppo praysto/tahrdee* |
| on time | in orario/puntuale<br>*een orahreeo/poontooahlay* |
| summertime (daylight saving) | ora legale<br>*orah laygahlay* |
| wintertime | ora invernale<br>*orah eenvayrnahlay* |

## .4 One, two, three...

| | | |
|---|---|---|
| 0 | zero | *dzayro* |
| 1 | uno | *oono* |
| 2 | due | *dooay* |
| 3 | tre | *tray* |
| 4 | quattro | *kwahttro* |
| 5 | cinque | *cheenkway* |
| 6 | sei | *sayèe* |
| 7 | sette | *sayttay* |
| 8 | otto | *otto* |
| 9 | nove | *novay* |
| 10 | dieci | *deeaychèe* |
| 11 | undici | *oondeechee* |
| 12 | dodici | *dodeechee* |
| 13 | tredici | *traydeechee* |
| 14 | quattordici | *kwahttordeechee* |
| 15 | quindici | *kweendeechee* |
| 16 | sedici | *saydeechee* |
| 17 | diciassette | *deechahssettay* |
| 18 | diciotto | *deecheeotto* |
| 19 | diciannove | *deechahnnovay* |
| 20 | venti | *vayntee* |
| 21 | ventuno | *vayntoono* |
| 22 | ventidue | *vaynteedooay* |
| 30 | trenta | *trayntah* |
| 31 | trentuno | *trayntoono* |
| 32 | trentadue | *trayntahdooay* |
| 40 | quaranta | *kwahrahntah* |
| 50 | cinquanta | *cheenkwahntah* |
| 60 | sessanta | *sayssahntah* |
| 70 | settanta | *sayttahntah* |
| 80 | ottanta | *ottahntah* |
| 90 | novanta | *novahntah* |
| 100 | cento | *chaynto* |
| 101 | centouno | *chayntooono* |
| 110 | centodieci | *chayntodeeaychee* |
| 120 | centoventi | *chayntovayntee* |
| 200 | duecento | *dooaychaynto* |
| 300 | trecento | *traychaynto* |
| 400 | quattrocento | *kwahttrochaynto* |
| 500 | cinquecento | *cheenkwaychaynto* |
| 600 | seicento | *saychaynto* |
| 700 | settecento | *sayttaychaynto* |
| 800 | ottocento | *ottochaynto* |
| 900 | novecento | *novaychaynto* |
| 1,000 | mille | *meellay* |
| 1,100 | millecento | *meellaychaynto* |
| 2,000 | duemila | *dooaymeelah* |
| 10,000 | diecimila | *deeaycheemeelah* |
| 100,000 | centomila | *chayntomeelah* |
| 1,000,000 | un milione | *oon meeleeonay* |

| | | |
|---|---|---|
| 1st | primo | *preemo* |
| 2nd | secondo | *saykondo* |
| 3rd | terzo | *tayrtzo* |
| 4th | quarto | *kwahrto* |
| 5th | quinto | *kweento* |
| 6th | sesto | *saysto* |
| 7th | settimo | *saytteemo* |
| 8th | ottavo | *ottahvo* |
| 9th | nono | *nono* |
| 10th | decimo | *daycheemo* |
| 11th | undicesimo | *oondeechayzeemo* |
| 12th | dodicesimo | *dodeechayzeemo* |
| 13th | tredicesimo | *traydeechayzeemo* |
| 14th | quattordicesimo | *kwahttordeechayzeemo* |
| 15th | quindicesimo | *kweendeechayzeemo* |
| 16th | sedicesimo | *saydeechayzeemo* |
| 17th | diciassettesimo | *deechahsayttayzeemo* |
| 18th | diciottesimo | *deechottayzeemo* |
| 19th | diciannovesimo | *deechahnovayzeemo* |
| 20th | ventesimo | *vayntayzeemo* |
| 21st | ventunesimo | *vayntoonayzeemo* |
| 22nd | ventiduesimo | *vaynteedooayzeemo* |
| 30th | trentesimo | *trahntayzeemo* |
| 100th | centesimo | *chayntayzeemo* |
| 1,000th | millesimo | *meellayzeemo* |
| once | una volta | *oonah voltah* |
| twice | due volte | *dooay voltay* |
| double | il doppio | *eel doppeeo* |
| triple | il triplo | *eel treeplo* |
| half | la metà | *lah maytah* |
| a quarter | un quarto | *oon kwahrto* |
| a third | un terzo | *oon tayrtzo* |
| some/a few | alcuni | *ahlkoonee* |

| | |
|---|---|
| 2 + 4 = 6 | due più quattro fa sei<br>*dooay peeoo kwahttro fah sayèe* |
| 4 - 2 = 2 | quattro meno due fa due<br>*kwahttro mayno dooay fah dooay* |
| 2 x 4 = 8 | due per quattro fa otto<br>*dooay payr kwahttro fah otto* |
| 4 ÷ 2 = 2 | quattro diviso due fa due<br>*kwahttro deeveezo dooay fah dooay* |
| even/odd | pari/dispari<br>*pahree/deesparee* |
| total | (in) totale<br>*(een) totahlay* |
| 6 x 9 | sei per nove<br>*sayèe payr novay* |

## 1.5 The weather

| | |
|---|---|
| Is the weather going to be good/bad? | Avremo bel/cattivo tempo?<br>*Avraymo bayl/kahtteevo taympo?* |
| Is it going to get colder/hotter? | Farà più freddo/più caldo?<br>*Fahrah peeoo frayddo/peeoo kahldo?* |
| What temperature is it going to be? | Quanti gradi ci saranno?<br>*Kwahntee grahdee chee sahrahnno?* |
| Is it going to rain? | Pioverà?<br>*Peeovayrah?* |
| Is there going to be a storm? | Ci sarà una tempesta?<br>*Chee sahrah oonah taympaystah?* |
| Is it going to snow? | Nevicherà?<br>*Nayveekayrah?* |
| Is it going to freeze? | Gelerà?<br>*Jaylayrah?* |
| Is the thaw setting in? | Sgelerà?<br>*Sjaylayrah?* |
| Is it going to be foggy? | Ci sarà la nebbia?<br>*Chee sahrah lah naybbeeah?* |
| Is there going to be a thunderstorm? | Avremo un temporale?<br>*Ahvraymo oon taymporahlay?* |
| The weather's changing | Il tempo cambia<br>*Eel taympo kahmbeeah* |
| It's going to be cold | Farà freddo<br>*Fahrah frayddo* |
| What's the weather going to be like today/ tomorrow? | Che tempo farà oggi/domani?<br>*Kay taympo fahrah odjee/domahnee?* |

afoso
**swelterings/muggy**

assolato
**sunny**

bello
**fine**

brina
**frost/frosty**

caldissimo
**very hot**

diluvio
**heavy rain**

forza del vento moderata/forte/ molto forte
**moderate/strong/ very strong winds**

freddo umido
**cold and damp**

fresco
**cool**

gelido
**bleak**

gelo
**frost**

gelo notturno
**overnight frost**

ghiaccio
**ice/icy**

giornata di sole
**sunny day**

... gradi (sotto/sopra zero)
**... degrees (below/above zero)**

grandine
**hail**

mite
**mild**

nebbia
**fog/foggy**

neve
**snow**

nuvolosità
**cloudiness**

ondata di caldo
**heatwave**

pioggia
**rain**

raffiche di vento
**gusts of wind**

rovescio di pioggia
**downpour**

sereno/nuvoloso/ coperto
**clear skies/cloudy/ overcast**

sereno
**fine/clear**

soffocante
**stifling**

tempesta
**storm**

umido
**humid**

uragano
**hurricaine**

vento
**wind**

ventoso
**windy**

##  .6 Here, there...

**See also 5.1 Asking for directions**

| | |
|---|---|
| here, over here / there, over there | qui, qua/lì, là<br>*kwee, kwah/lee, lah* |
| somewhere/nowhere | da qualche parte/da nessuna parte<br>*dah kwahlkay pahrtay/dah nayssoonah pahrtay* |
| everywhere | dappertutto<br>*dahppayrtootto* |
| far away/nearby | lontano/vicino<br>*lontahno/veecheeno* |
| (on the) right/(on the) left | a destra/a sinistra<br>*ah daystrah/ah seeneestrah* |
| to the right/left of | a destra di/a sinistra di<br>*ah daystrah dee/ah seeneestrah dee* |
| straight ahead | dritto<br>*dreetto* |
| via | per<br>*payr* |
| in/to | in/a<br>*een/ah* |
| on | su/sopra<br>*soo/soprah* |
| under | sotto<br>*sotto* |
| against | contro<br>*contro* |
| opposite/facing | di fronte a<br>*dee frontay ah* |
| next to | accanto a<br>*ahkkahnto ah* |
| near | presso/vicino a<br>*praysso/veecheeno ah* |
| in front of | davanti a/dinanzi a<br>*dahvahntee ah/deenahnzee ah* |
| in the centre | al centro<br>*al chayntro* |
| forward | avanti<br>*ahvahntee* |
| down | (in) giù<br>*(een) joo* |
| up | (in) su<br>*(een) soo* |
| inside | dentro<br>*dayntro* |
| outside | fuori<br>*fworee* |
| behind | (in)dietro<br>*(een) deeayhtro* |
| at the front | davanti<br>*dahvahntee* |
| at the back/in line | in fondo/in fila<br>*een fondo/een feelah* |
| in the north | nel nord<br>*nayl nord* |

| | |
|---|---|
| to the south | al sud<br>*ahl sood* |
| from the west | dall'ovest<br>*dahllovayst* |
| from the east | dall'est<br>*dahllayst* |
| to the...of | a... di<br>*ah... dee* |

##  .7 What does that sign say?

***See 5.4 Traffic signs***

a noleggio
for hire
acqua calda/fredda
hot/cold water
acqua (non) potabile
(no) drinking water
affittasi
for rent
albergo
hotel
alt
stop
alta tensione
high voltage
aperto
open
attenti al cane
beware of the dog
attenzione
danger
biglietteria
ticket office
cambio
exchange
carabinieri
police
cassa
cash desk/pay here
chiuso (per ferie/restauro)
closed (for holiday/ refurbishment)
completo
full
divieto di caccia/ pesca
no hunting/fishing
entrata
entrance
esaurito
sold out
freno d'emergenza
hand brake
fuori uso
not in use
gabinetti
lavatories/toilets
guasto
out of order
in vendita
for sale
informazioni
information
ingresso (libero)
entrance (free)
non disturbare/ toccare
please do not disturb/touch
occupato
engaged
orario
timetable
ospedale
hospital
pedoni
pedestrians
pericolo (d'incendio/ di morte)
danger/fire hazard/ danger to life
polizia stradale
traffic police
pronto soccorso
first aid/accident and emergency (hospital)
riservato
reserved
sala d'attesa
waiting room
scala di sicurezza/mobile
fire escape/escalator
spingere
push
tirare
pull
ufficio informazioni turistiche
tourist information bureau
ufficio postale
post office
uscita (di emergenza)
(emergency) exit
vendesi
for sale
vernice fresca
wet paint
vietato fumare/ gettare rifiuti
no smoking/no litter
vietato l'accesso/ l'ingresso
no access/no entry
vigili del fuoco
fire brigade
vigili urbani
(municipal) police

## 1.8 Telephone alphabet

Pronouncing the alphabet, e.g. A as in Ancona

| | | | |
|---|---|---|---|
| a | *ah* | come Ancona | *komay Ankonah* |
| b | *bee* | come Bologna | *komay Bolonyah* |
| c | *chee* | come Como | *komay Komo* |
| d | *dee* | come Domodossola | *komay Domodossolah* |
| e | *ay* | come Empoli | *komay Empolee* |
| f | *ayffay* | come Firenze | *komay Feeraynzay* |
| g | *jee* | come Genova | *komay Jaynovah* |
| h | *ahkkah* | come Hotel | *komay Hotayl* |
| i | *ee* | come Imola | *komay Eemolah* |
| j | *ee loongo* | come Jersey | *komay Jayrsay* |
| k | *kahppah* | come Kursaal | *komay Koorsaal* |
| l | *ayllay* | come Livorno | *komay Leevorno* |
| m | *aymmay* | come Milano | *komay Meelahno* |
| n | *aynnay* | come Napoli | *komay Nahpolee* |
| o | *o* | come Otranto | *komay Otrahnto* |
| p | *pee* | come Padova | *komay Pahdovah* |
| q | *koo* | come Quarto | *komay Kwahrto* |
| r | *ayrray* | come Roma | *komay Romah* |
| s | *ayssay* | come Savona | *komay Sahvonah* |
| t | *tee* | come Torino | *komay Toreeno* |
| u | *oo* | come Udine | *komay Oodeenay* |
| v | *voo* | come Venezia | *komay Vaynaytzyah* |
| w | *doppeeovoo or voodoppeeo* | come Washington | *komay Washington* |
| x | *eex* | come Xeres | *komay Xayrays* |
| y | *eepseelon* | come York, yacht | *komay York, yahcht* |
| z | *dzayhtah* | come Zara | *komay Dzahrah* |

## 1.9 Personal details

| | |
|---|---|
| surname | cognome<br>*koneeomay* |
| first/forename | nome<br>*nomay* |
| initials | iniziali<br>*eeneetzeeahlee* |
| address (street/number) | indirizzo (via/numero)<br>*eendeereetzo (veeah/noomahro)* |
| post code/town | codice postale/residenza<br>*kodeechay postahlay/rayseedayntzah* |
| sex (male/female) | sesso (m/f)<br>*saysso (m/f)* |
| nationality/citizenship | nazionalità/cittadinanza<br>*nahtzeeonahleetah/cheettahdeenahntzah* |
| date of birth | data di nascita<br>*dahtah dee nahsheetah* |
| place of birth | luogo di nascita<br>*loo-ogo dee nahsheetah* |
| occupation | professione<br>*profaysseeonay* |
| marital status | stato civile<br>*stahto cheeveelay* |

| | |
|---|---|
| married, single | coniugato/a, celibe (m) nubile (f)<br>*konyoogahto/tah, chayleebay/ noobeelay* |
| widowed | vedovo (m), vedova (f)<br>*vaydovo, vaydovah* |
| (number of) children | (numero di) figli<br>*(noomahro dee) feelly* |
| passport/identity card/driving licence number | numero del passaporto/della carta di identità/della patente<br>*noomayro dayl pahssahporto/dayllah cahrtah deedaynteetah/dayllah pahtayntay* |
| place and date of issue | luogo e data di rilascio<br>*loo-ogo ay dahtah dee reelahshyo* |
| signature | firma<br>*feermah* |

# Courtesies

# Courtesies

● **It is usual in Italy** to shake hands on meeting and parting company. Female friends and relatives may kiss each other on both cheeks when meeting and parting company. For men, this is also quite usual. It is also polite to say *Signore* and *Signora* quite systematically as part of a greeting, i.e. *Buongiorno/arrivederLa, signora.*



## 2.1 Greetings

| | |
|---|---|
| Hello/Good morning Mr Williams | Buongiorno signor Williams<br>*Bwonjorno seeneeor Williams* |
| Hello/Good morning Mrs Jones | Buongiorno signora Jones<br>*Bwonjorno sineeorah Jones* |
| Hello, Peter | Ciao Peter<br>*Chaho Peter* |
| Hi, Helen | Ciao Helen<br>*Chaho Helen* |
| Good morning, madam | Buongiorno signora<br>*Bwonjorno seeneeorah* |
| Good afternoon, sir | Buongiorno signore<br>*Bwonjorno seeneeoray* |
| Good afternoon/evening | Buona sera<br>*Bwona sayrah* |
| Hello/Good morning | Buongiorno<br>*Bwonjorno* |
| How are you?/How are things? | Come va?<br>*Komay vah?* |
| Fine, thank you, and you? | Bene, grazie, e Lei?<br>*Baynay, grahtzeeay, ay layee?* |
| Very well, and you? | Benissimo, e Lei?<br>*Bayneesseemo, ay layee?* |
| In excellent health/ In great shape | In ottima forma<br>*Een otteemah formah* |
| So-so | Così così<br>*Cozee cozee* |
| Not very well | Non molto bene<br>*Non molto baynay* |
| Not bad | Non c'è male<br>*Non chay mahlay* |
| I'm going to leave | Me ne vado<br>*May nay vahdo* |
| I have to be going someone's waiting for me | Devo andarmene. Mi aspettano<br>*Dayvo ahndahrmaynay. Mee ahspettahno* |
| Goodbye | Ciao!<br>*Chaho!* |
| Good-bye/Good-bye (formal)/See you later | Arrivederci/ArrivederLa/Ci vediamo<br>*Ahrreevaydayrchee/ahrreevaydayrlah/chee vaydeeahmo* |
| See you soon | A presto<br>*Ah praysto* |
| See you later | A più tardi<br>*Ah peeoo tahrdee* |
| See you in a little while | A fra poco<br>*Ah frah poko* |

| | |
|---|---|
| Sweet dreams | Sogni d'oro<br>*Sonyee doro* |
| Good night | Buona notte<br>*Bwonah nottay* |
| All the best | Tante belle cose<br>*Tahntay bayllay kozay* |
| Have fun | Buon divertimento<br>*Bwon deevayrteemaynto* |
| Good luck | Buona fortuna/in bocca al lupo<br>*Bwonah fortoonah/een bokkah al loopo* |
| Have a nice holiday | Buone vacanze/buone ferie<br>*Bwonay vahkahntzay/bwonay fayreeay* |
| Bon voyage/Have a good trip | Buon viaggio<br>*Bwon veeahdjo* |
| Thank you, the same to you | Grazie, altrettanto<br>*Grahtzeeay, ahltrayttahnto* |
| Say hello to/Give my regards to (formal).... | Mi saluti...<br>*Mee sahlootee...* |
| Say hello to (informal) | Salutami...<br>*Sahlootahmee...* |

## 2.2 How to ask a question

| | |
|---|---|
| Who? | Chi?<br>*Kee?* |
| Who's that?/Who is it?/Who's there? | Chi è?<br>*Kee ay?* |
| What? | Che (cosa)?<br>*Kay (kosah)?* |
| What is there to see? | Che c'è da vedere?<br>*Kay chay dah vaydayray?* |
| What category of hotel is it? | Che tipo di albergo è?<br>*Kay teepo dee ahlbayrgo ay?* |
| Where? | Dove?<br>*Dovay?* |
| Where's the toilet/bathroom? | Dov'è il bagno?<br>*Dovay ay eel bahneeo?* |
| Where are you going? (formal) | Dove va?<br>*Dovay vah?* |
| Where are you from? | Da dove viene?<br>*Dah dovay veeayhnay?* |
| What?/How? | Come?<br>*Komay?* |
| How far is that? | Quanto è lontano?<br>*Kwahnto ay lontahno?* |
| How long does that take? | Quanto tempo ci vorrà?<br>*Kwahnto taympo chee vorrah?* |
| How long is the trip? | Quanto tempo durerà il viaggio?<br>*Kwahnto taympo doorayrah eel veeahdjo?* |
| How much? | Quanto?<br>*Kwahnto?* |
| How much is this? | Quanto costa?<br>*Kwahnto kostah?* |
| What time is it? | Che ore sono?<br>*Kay oray sono?* |
| Which one/s? | Quale?/Quali?<br>*Kwahlay?/Kwahlee?* |

Which glass is mine? _____ Qual è il mio bicchiere?
*Kwahlay eel meeo beekkeeayray?*

When? _____ Quando?
*Kwahndo?*

When are you leaving? (formal) _____ Quando parte?
*Kwahndo pahrtay?*

Why? _____ Perchè?
*Payrkay?*

Could you...? (formal) _____ Potrebbe...?
*Potraybbay..?*

Could you help me/give me a hand please? _____ Potrebbe darmi una mano, per piacere?
*Potraybbay dahrmee oonah mahno, payr peeahchayray?*

Could you point that out to me/show me please? Potrebbe indicarmelo?
*Potraybbay eendeekahrmayhlo?*

Could you come with me, please? _____ Potrebbe accompagnarmi, per favore?
*Potraybbay ahkkompahnyahrmee, payr fahvoray?*

Could you reserve/book me some tickets please? _____ Mi potrebbe prenotare dei biglietti, per piacere?
*Mee potraybbay praynotahray day beellyayttee, payr peeahchayray?*

Could you recommend another hotel? _____ Saprebbe consigliarmi un altro albergo?
*Sahpraybbay konseellyahrmee oonahltro ahlbayrgo?*

Do you know...? (formal) _____ Saprebbe...?
*Saprebbay...?*

Do you know whether...? _____ Sa se...?
*Sah say...?*

Do you have...? (formal) _____ Ha...?
*Ah...?*

Do you have a.... for me? _____ Ha un/una...per me?
*Ah oon/oona.....payr may?*

Do you have a vegetarian dish, please? _____ Ha per caso un piatto vegetariano/senza carne?
*Ah payr kahzo oon pyahtto vayjaytahryahno/saynzah kahrnay?*

I would like... _____ Vorrei...
*Vorrayee...*

I'd like a kilo of apples, please _____ Vorrei un chilo di mele
*Vorrayee oon keelo dee mayhlay*

Can/May I? _____ Posso...?
*Posso...?*

Can/May I take this away? _____ Posso portare via questo?
*Posso portahray veeah kwaysto?*

Can I smoke here? _____ Si può fumare qui?
*See pwo foomahray kwee?*

Could I ask you something? _____ Posso farLe una domanda?
*Posso fahrlay oonah domahndah?*

## 2.3 How to reply

|  |  |
|---|---|
| Yes, of course | Sì certo<br>*See chayrto* |
| No, I'm sorry | No, mi dispiace<br>*No, mee deespeeahchay* |
| Yes, what can I do for you? | Sì, che cosa desidera?<br>*See, kay kosah dayzeederah?* |
| Just a moment, please | Un attimo, per favore<br>*Oon attymo payr fahvoray* |
| No, I don't have time now | No, purtroppo ora non ho tempo<br>*No, poortroppo orah non o taympo* |
| No, that's impossible | No, non è possibile<br>*No, non ay posseebeelay* |
| I think so/I think that's absolutely right | Credo di sì/Credo proprio di sì<br>*Kraydo dee see/Kraydo propreeo dee see* |
| I think so too/I agree | Lo penso anch'io<br>*Lo paynso ahnkeeo* |
| I hope so too | Lo spero anch'io<br>*Lo spayro ankeeo* |
| No, not at all/Absolutely not | No, niente affatto<br>*No, neeayntay ahffahtto* |
| No, no-one | No, nessuno<br>*No, nayssoono* |
| No, nothing | No, niente<br>*No, neeayntay* |
| That's right | Esatto<br>*Ezahtto* |
| Something's wrong | C'è qualcosa che non va<br>*Chay kwahlkosah kahy non vah* |
| I agree (don't agree) | (Non) sono d'accordo<br>*(Non) sono dahkkordo* |
| OK/it's fine | Va bene<br>*Vah bayhnay* |
| OK, all right | D'accordo<br>*Dahkkordo* |
| Perhaps/maybe | Forse<br>*Forsay* |
| I don't know | Non lo so<br>*Non lo so* |

## 2.4 Thank you

|  |  |
|---|---|
| Thank you | Grazie<br>*Grahtzeeay* |
| You're welcome | Di niente/nulla<br>*Dee neeayntay/noollah* |
| Thank you very much/ Many thanks | Mille grazie<br>*Meellay grahtzeeay* |
| Very kind of you | Molto gentile<br>*Molto jaynteelay* |
| My pleasure | E' stato un piacere<br>*Ay stahto oon peeahchayray* |
| I enjoyed it very much | Mi è piaciuto moltissimo<br>*Mee ay peeacheeooto molteesseemo* |
| Thank you for... | La ringrazio di...<br>*Lah reengrahtzeeo dee...* |

| | |
|---|---|
| You shouldn't have/That was so kind of you | E stato veramente gentile/da parte sua<br>*Ay stahto vayrahmayntay jaynteelay/dah pahrtay sooah* |
| Don't mention it! | Ma si figuri!<br>*Mah see feegoory!* |
| That's all right | Prego<br>*Praygo* |

## 2.5 Sorry

| | |
|---|---|
| Excuse me/pardon me/sorry (formal) | Scusi!<br>*Skoozee!* |
| Excuse me/pardon me/sorry (informal) | Scusa!<br>*Skoozah!* |
| Sorry, I didn't know that.... | Scusi, ma non sapevo che...<br>*Skoozee, mah non sahpayvo kay...* |
| Excuse/pardon me (formal) | Mi scusi<br>*Mee skoozee* |
| I do apologise (formal/informal) | La/ti prego di scusarmi<br>*Lah/tee praygo dee scoosahrmee* |
| I'm sorry | Mi dispiace<br>*Mee deespeeahchay* |
| I didn't mean it/It was an accident | Non l'ho fatto apposta<br>*Non lo fahtto appostah* |
| That's all right/Don't worry about it (formal) | Non si preoccupi<br>*Non see prayokkoopee* |
| Never mind/Forget it (informal) | Non importa<br>*Non eemportah* |
| It could happen to anyone | Può succedere a tutti<br>*Pwo sootchaydayray ah tootty* |

## 2.6 What do you think?

| | |
|---|---|
| Which do you prefer/like best (formal) | Cosa preferisce?<br>*Kosah prayfayreeshay?* |
| What do you think? (informal) | Che ne pensi?<br>*Kay nay pensee?* |
| Don't you like dancing? (formal/informal) | Non le/ti piace ballare?<br>*Non lay/tee peeahchay bahllahray?* |
| I don't mind | Per me è uguale<br>*Payr may ay oogwahlay* |
| Well done! (m.sing/f.sing/m.plu/f.plu) | Bravo/brava/bravi/brave!<br>*Brahvo/brahvah/brahvee/brahvay!* |
| Not bad! | Niente male!<br>*Neeayntay mahlay!* |
| Great!/Marvellous! | Che meraviglia!<br>*Kay mayrahveellyah!* |
| Wonderful! | Stupendo!<br>*Stoopayndo!* |
| How lovely! | Che bello!<br>*Kay bayllo!* |
| I am pleased for you (formal/informal) | Mi fa piacere per Lei/te<br>*Mee fah peeahchayay payr layee/tay* |
| I'm (not very happy) delighted to/with... | (Non) sono molto contento/a di...<br>*(Non) sono molto contaynto/ah dee...* |
| It's really nice here! | È proprio un bel posto<br>*Ay propreeo oon bayl posto* |

| | |
|---|---|
| How nice! | Che bello!<br>*Kay bayllo!* |
| How nice for you! | Mi fa piacere per Lei/te<br>*Mee fah peeahchayray payr Layee/tay* |
| I'm (not) very happy with... | (Non) sono molto contento/a di<br>*(Non) sono molto kontaynto/ah dee* |
| I'm glad that.... | Sono contento che...<br>*Sono kontaynto kay...* |
| I'm having a great time | Mi sto divertendo moltissimo<br>*Mee sto deevayrtayndo molteesseemo* |
| I can't wait 'til tomorrow /I'm looking forward to tomorrow | Non vedo l'ora che sia domani<br>*Non vaydo lorah kay seeah domahny* |
| I hope it works out | Spero che vada bene<br>*Spayhro kay vahdah bayhnay* |
| How awful! | Che brutto!<br>*Kay brootto!* |
| It's horrible | E' orribile<br>*Ay orreebeelay* |
| That's ridiculous! | È ridicolo!<br>*Ay reedeekolo!* |
| That's terrible! | Ma è terribile!<br>*Mah ay tayrreebeelay!* |
| What a pity/shame! | Che peccato!<br>*Kay paykkahto!* |
| How disgusting! | Che schifo!<br>*Kay skeefo!* |
| What a load of rubbish/How silly! | Che sciocchezze!<br>*Kay shokkaytzay!* |
| I don't like it/them | Non mi piace.../Non mi piacciono...<br>*Non mee peeahchay.../Non mee peeahcheeono...* |
| I'm bored to death | Sto morendo di noia<br>*Sto morayndo dee noeeah* |
| I'm fed up | Mi sono stufato/a<br>*Mee sono stoofahto/ah* |
| This is no good | Questo non va bene<br>*Kwaysto non vah baynay* |
| This is not what I expected | Mi aspettavo una cosa diversa<br>*Mee ahspayttahvo oonah kosah deevayrsah* |

# Conversation

# Conversation

## 3.1 I beg your pardon?



|  |  |
|---|---|
| I don't speak any/ I speak a little... | Non parlo/Parlo un po' di...<br>*Non parlo/Parlo oon po dee...* |
| I'm English | Sono inglese<br>*Sono eenglaysay* |
| I'm Scottish | Sono scozzese<br>*Sono skotzaysay* |
| I'm Irish | Sono irlandese<br>*Sono eerlahndaysay* |
| I'm Welsh | Sono gallese<br>*Sono gahllaysay* |
| Do you speak English? (formal) | Lei parla inglese?<br>*Layee pahrlah eenglaysay?* |
| Is there anyone who speaks...? | C'è qualcuno che parla...?<br>*Chay kwahlkoono kay pahrlah...?* |
| I beg your pardon/ What? | Come?<br>*Komay?* |
| I (don't) understand | (Non) capisco<br>*(Non) kahpeesko* |
| Do you understand me? (formal) | Mi capisce?<br>*Mee kahpeeshay?* |
| Could you repeat that, please? | Potrebbe ripetermelo?<br>*Potraybbay reepayhtayrmaylo?* |
| Could you speak more slowly, please? | Potrebbe parlare un po' più lentamente?<br>*Potraybbay pahrlahray oon po peeoo layntahmayntay?* |
| What does that mean?/that word mean? | Che cosa significa/Che cosa significa quella parola?<br>*Kay kosah seeneefeekah/Kay kosah seeneefeekah kwayllah pahrolah?* |
| It's more or less the same as... | E' più o meno lo stesso di...?<br>*Ay peeoo o mayno lo staysso dee..* |
| Could you write that down for me, please? | Potrebbe scrivermelo?<br>*Potraybbay skreevayrmaylo?* |
| Could you spell that for me, please? | Come si scrive?<br>*Komay see skreevay?* |

***(See 1.8 Telephone alphabet)***

|  |  |
|---|---|
| Could you point that out in this phrase book, please? | Potrebbe indicarmelo in questo frasario?<br>*Potraybbay eendeekahrmaylo een kwaysto frahzahreeo?* |
| Just a minute, I'll look it up | Un attimo che lo cerco<br>*Oon ahtteemo kay lo chayrko* |
| I can't find the word/the sentence | Non riesco a trovare la parola/la frase<br>*Non reeaysko ah trovahray lah pahrolah/lah frahzay* |
| How do you say that in...? | Come si dice in...?<br>*Komay see deechay een...?* |
| How do you pronounce that? | Come si pronuncia?<br>*Komay see pronoonchah?* |

## 3.2 Introductions



| | |
|---|---|
| May I introduce myself? | Permette che mi presenti?<br>*Payrmayttay kay mee praysayntee?* |
| My name's... | Mi chiamo...<br>*Mee keeahmo...* |
| I'm... | Sono...<br>*Sono...* |
| What's your name? (formal/informal)... | Lei, come si chiama?/Come ti chiami?<br>*Lay, komay see keeahmah?/Komay tee keeahmee?* |
| May I introduce...? (formal/informal)... | Permette, Le presento.../Permetti, ti presento...<br>*Payrmayttay, lay praysaynto.../Payrmayttee, tee praysaynto...* |
| This is my wife/husband (formal/informal) | Le/ti presento mia moglie/mio marito<br>*Lay/tee praysaynto meeah mollyay/meeo mahreeto* |
| This is my daughter/son (formal/informal) | Le/ti presento mia figlia/mio figlio<br>*Lay/tee presento meeah feellyah/meeo feellyo* |
| This is my mother/father (formal/informal) | Le/ti presento mia madre/mio padre<br>*Lay/tee praysaynto meeah mahdray/meeo pahdray* |
| This is my fiancée/fiancé (formal/informal) | Le/ti presento la mia fidanzata/il mio fidanzato<br>*Lay/tee praysaynto lah meeah feedahntzahtah/eel meeo feedahntzahto* |
| This is my friend (f/m) (formal/informal) | Le/ti presento un'amica mia/un amico mio<br>*Lay/tee praysaynto oonahmeekah meeah/oonahmeeko meeo* |
| How do you do | Piacere<br>*Peeahchayray* |
| Hi, pleased to meet you (informal) | Ciao, piacere di conoscerti<br>*Chahoo, peeahchayray dee konoshayrtee* |
| Pleased to meet you (formal) | Piacere di conoscerLa<br>*Peeahchayray dee konoshayrlah* |
| Where are you from? (formal/informal) | Lei, di dov'è?/Di dove sei?<br>*Layèe dee dovay ay?/Dee dovay sayee?* |
| I'm English | Sono inglese<br>*Sono eenglaysay* |
| What city do you live in? | In quale città abita?<br>*Een kwahlay cheettah ahbeetah?* |
| In...near.... | Abito a... vicino a...<br>*Ahbeeto ah... veecheeno ah...* |
| Have you been here long? | E' molto che sta qui?<br>*Ay molto kay stah kwee?* |
| A few days | Qualche giorno<br>*Kwahlkay jorno* |
| How long are you staying here? | Quanto tempo rimarrà?<br>*Kwahnto taympo reemahrrah?* |
| We're (probably) leaving tomorrow/ in two weeks | Partiremo (probabilmente) domani/fra due settimane<br>*Pahrtyraymo (probahbeelmayntay) domahny/frah dooay sayttymahnay* |
| Where are you (m/f) staying? | Dov'è alloggiato/a?<br>*Dovay ay ahllodjahto/ah?* |

| | |
|---|---|
| I'm staying in a hotel/an apartment | Sono alloggiato in un albergo/ appartamento<br>*Sono ahllodjahto een oon ahlbayrgo/ahppahrtahmaynto* |
| At a campsite | Sono in campeggio<br>*Sono een kahmpaydjo* |
| I'm staying with friends/relatives | Sono ospite di amici/sono a casa di parenti<br>*Sono ospeetay dee ahmeechee/sono ah kasa dee pahrayntee* |
| Are you (m/f) here on your own? Are you here with your family? | E' da solo/a?/E' con la Sua famiglia?<br>*Ay dah solo/ah?/Ay con lah sooah fahmeellyah?* |
| I'm on my own | Sono da solo/a<br>*Sono dah solo/ah* |
| I'm with my partner/wife/husband | Sono con il mio partner/la mia partner/mia moglie/mio marito<br>*Sono con eel meeo pahrtnayr/lah meeah pahrtnayr/meeah mollyay/meeo mahreeto* |
| – with my family | Sono con la mia famiglia<br>*Sono con lah meeah fahmeellyah* |
| – with relatives | Sono con i miei parenti<br>*Sono con ee meeayee pahrayntee* |
| – with a friend/friends (m.sing/f.sing/m. plu/ f.plu) | Sono con un amico/un'amica/degli amici/delle amiche<br>*Sono con oonahmeeko/oonahmeekah/ daylyee ahmeechee/daylly ahmeekay* |
| Are you married? (m/f) | Lei è sposato/a?<br>*Layèe ay sposahto/ah?* |
| Are you engaged?/ Do you have a steady boy/ girlfriend? | È fidanzato/È fidanzata?<br>*Ay feedahntzahto/Ay feedahntzahtah?* |
| That's none of your business (formal/informal) | Questo non La/ti riguarda per niente<br>*Kwaysto non lah/tee reegwahrdah payr nee-ayntay* |
| I'm married (m/f) | Sono sposato/a<br>*Sono spozahto/ah* |
| I'm single (m. only) | Sono scapolo<br>*Sono skahpolo* |
| I'm not married (m/f) | Non sono sposato/a<br>*Non sono sposahto/ah* |
| I'm separated (m/f) | Sono separato/a<br>*Sono saypahrahto/ah* |
| I'm divorced (m/f) | Sono divorziato/a<br>*Sono deevortzeeahto/ah* |
| I'm a widow/widower | Sono vedova/o<br>*Sono vaydovah/o* |
| I live alone (m/f)/with someone | Vivo da solo/a/Vivo con il mio partner/la mia partner<br>*Veevo dah solo/ah/Veevo con eel meeo pahrtnayr/lah meeah pahrtnayr* |
| Do you have any children/grandchildren? | Ha figli/nipoti?<br>*Ah feelly/neepotee?* |
| How old are (formal/informal) you? | Quanti anni ha/hai?<br>*Kwahnty ahnnee ah/ahee?* |
| How old is she/he? | Quanti anni ha (lei/lui)?<br>*Kwahnty ahnnee ah (lahee/looee)?* |

| | |
|---|---|
| I'm... (years old) | Ho...anni<br>*O...ahnnee* |
| She's/he's...(years old) | Ha...anni<br>*Ah...ahnnee* |
| What do you do for a living? (formal/informal) | Che lavoro fa/fai??<br>*Kay lahvoro faah?/faee?* |
| I work in an office | Lavoro in ufficio<br>*Lahvoro een ooffeecho* |
| I'm a student (m/f) | Sono uno studente/una studentessa<br>*Sono oono stoodayntay/oona stoodayntayssah* |
| I am unemployed (m/f) | Sono disoccupato/a<br>*Sono deesokkoopahto/ah* |
| I'm retired | Sono pensionato/a<br>*Sono paynseeonahto/ah* |
| I'm on a disability pension | Sono invalido/a al lavoro<br>*Sono eenvahleedo/ah ahl lahvoro* |
| I'm a housewife | Sono casalinga<br>*Sono kahsahleengah* |
| Do you like your job? (formal/informal) | Le/ti piace il Suo/tuo lavoro?<br>*Lay/tee peeahchay eel soo-o/too-o lahvoro?* |
| Most of the time | Per lo più sì<br>*Payr lo peeoo see* |
| Mostly I do, but I prefer holidays | Il più delle volte sì, però le vacanze mi piacciono di più<br>*Eel peeoo dayllay voltay see, payro lay vahkahntzay mee peeahchono dee peeoo* |

## 3.3 Starting/ending a conversation

| | |
|---|---|
| Could I ask you something? (formal/informal) | Posso chiederLe/ti una cosa?<br>*Posso keeaydayrlay/tee oonah kosah?* |
| Excuse/Pardon me (formal/informal) | Mi scusi/scusami<br>*Mee skoozee/skoozahmee* |
| Could you help me please? | Scusi, mi può aiutare?<br>*Skoozee, mee pwo aheeootahray?* |
| Yes, what's the problem? | Sì, che cosa c'è?<br>*See, kay kosah chay?* |
| What can I do for you? | Di che cosa ha bisogno?<br>*Dee kay kosah ah beezoneeo?* |
| Sorry, I don't have time now | Mi dispiace, non ho tempo<br>*Mee deespeeahchay, non o taympo* |
| Do you have a light? (formal/informal) | Ha/hai da accendere?<br>*Ah/ay dah ahtchayndayhray?* |
| May I join you? | Posso farLe compagnia?<br>*Posso fahrlay compahnee-ah?* |
| Could you take a picture of me/us? | Mi/ci potrebbe fare una foto?<br>*Mee/chee potraybbay fahray oonah photo?* |
| Leave me alone (formal/informal) | Mi lasci/lasciami in pace<br>*Mee lahshee/Lahshahmee een pahchay* |
| Get lost (formal/informal) | Se ne vada/Vattene<br>*Say nay vahdah/Vahttenay* |
| Go away or I'll scream | Se non se ne va subito, strillo<br>*Say non say nay vah soobeeto, streello* |

## 3.4 Congratulations and condolences

|  |  |
|---|---|
| Happy birthday/many happy returns/happy name day | Tanti auguri, buon compleanno/buon onomastico<br>*Tahntee owgooree, bwon complayahnno/bwon onomahsteeko* |
| Please accept my condolences. | Le mie condoglianze<br>*Lay meeay condollyahnzay* |
| My deepest sympathy | Mi dispiace moltissimo<br>*Mee deespeeahchay molteesseemo* |

## 3.5 A chat about the weather

***See also 1.5 The weather***

|  |  |
|---|---|
| It's so hot/cold today! | Che caldo/freddo oggi!<br>*Kay kahldo/frayddo odjee!* |
| Isn't it a lovely day? | Che bella giornata!<br>*Kay bayllah jornahtah!* |
| It's so windy/ what a storm! | Che vento/temporale!<br>*Kay vaynto/taymporahlay!* |
| All that rain/snow! | Che pioggia/neve!<br>*Kay peeodjah/nayhvay!* |
| It's so foggy! | Che nebbia!<br>*Kay naybbeeah!* |
| Has the weather been like this for long? | E' da parecchio che avete questo tempo?<br>*Ay dah pahraykkeeo kay ahvaytay kwaysto taympo?* |
| Is it always this hot/cold here? | Fa sempre tanto caldo/freddo qui?<br>*Fah saympray tahnto kahldo/frayddo kwee?* |
| Is it always this dry/ humid here? | E' sempre tanto secco/umido qui?<br>*Ay saympray tahnto saykko/oomeedo kwee?* |

## 3.6 Hobbies

|  |  |
|---|---|
| Do you have any hobbies?(formal/informal) | Ha/hai qualche hobby?<br>*Ah/ay kwahlkay obby?* |
| I like knitting/ reading/photography/ DIY | Mi piace lavorare a maglia/leggere/la fotografia/il fai-da-te<br>*Mee peeahchay lahvoraray ah mahllyah/ledjayray/lah fotograhfeeah/eell fahee dah tay* |
| I enjoy listening to music | Mi piace ascoltare la musica<br>*Mee peeahchay ahskoltahray lah moozeekah* |
| I play the guitar/the piano | Suono la chitarra/il pianoforte<br>*Swono lah keetahrrah/eel peeahnofortay* |
| I like the cinema | Mi piace andare al cinema<br>*Mee peeahchay ahndahray ahl cheenaymah* |
| I like travelling/playing sport/going fishing/going for a walk | Mi piace viaggiare/fare dello sport/andare a pesca/fare passeggiate<br>*Mee peeahchay veeahdjahray/fahray dayllo sport/ahndahray ah payskah/fahray pahssaydjahtay* |

## 3.7 Being the host(ess)

***See also 4 Eating out***

| | |
|---|---|
| Can I offer you a drink? (formal/informal) | Le/ti posso offrire qualcosa da bere?<br>*Lay/tee posso offreeray kwahlkosah dah bayray?* |
| What would you like to drink? (formal/informal) | Cosa beve?/Cosa bevi?<br>*Kozah bayvay?/Kozah bayvee?* |
| Something non-alcoholic, please. | Vorrei una bibita analcolica<br>*Vorrayèe oonah beebeetah ahnahlkoleekah* |
| Would you like a cigarette/cigar | Vuole una sigaretta/un sigaro?<br>*Vwolay oonah seegahrayttah/oon seegahro?* |
| I don't smoke | Non fumo<br>*Non foomo* |

## 3.8 Invitations

| | |
|---|---|
| Are you doing anything tonight? (formal/informal) | Ha/hai qualcosa da fare stasera?<br>*Ah/ay kwahlkosah dah fahray stahsayhrah?* |
| Do you have any plans for today/this afternoon/tonight? (formal/informal) | Che intende/intendi fare oggi/questo pomeriggio/stasera?<br>*Kay eentaynday/eentayndee fahray odjee/kwaysto pomayreedjo/stahsayrah?* |
| Would you like to go out with me? (formal/informal) | Le/ti piacerebbe uscire con me?<br>*Lay/tee peeahchayraybbay oosheeray con may?* |
| Would you like to go dancing with me? (formal/informal) | Le/ti piacerebbe andare a ballare con me?<br>*Lay/tee peeahcherebbay ahndaray ah bahllahray con may?* |
| Would you like to have lunch/dinner with me? (formal/informal) | Le/ti piacerebbe venire a pranzo/a cena con me?<br>*Lay/tee peeahchayraybbay vayneeray ah prahnzo/ah chaynah con may?* |
| Would you like to come to the beach with me? (formal/informal) | Le/ti piacerebbe venire alla spiaggia con me?<br>*Lay/tee peeahchayraybbay vayneeray allah spee-ahdjah con may?* |
| Would you like to come into town with us? (formal/informal) | Le/ti piacerebbe venire in città con noi?<br>*Lay/tee peeahchayraybbay vayneeray een cheettah con noee?* |
| Would you like to come and see some friends with us? (formal/informal) | Le/ti piacerebbe venire con noi a trovare degli amici?<br>*Lay/tee peeahchayraybbay veneeray con noee ah trovahray daylly ahmeechee?* |
| Shall we dance? | Balliamo?<br>*Bahlleeahmo?* |
| – sit at the bar? | Ci sediamo al bar?<br>*Chee saydeeahmo ahl bahr?* |
| – get something to drink? | Beviamo qualcosa?<br>*Beveeahmo kwahlkosah?* |
| – go for a walk/drive? | Vogliamo fare due passi? Facciamo un giro in macchina?<br>*Vollyahmo fahray dooay pahssee?*<br>*Fahtcheeahmo oon jeero een mahkkeenah?* |
| Yes, all right | Sí, va bene<br>*See, vah baynay* |

| | |
|---|---|
| Good idea | E' una buona idea<br>*Ay oonah bwonah eedayah* |
| No thank you | No grazie<br>*No, grahtzeeay* |
| Maybe later | Più tardi, forse<br>*Peeoo tahrdy, forsay* |
| I don't feel like it | Non mi va<br>*Non mee vah* |
| I don't have time | Purtroppo non ho tempo<br>*Poortroppo non o taympo* |
| I already have a date | Ho già un altro appuntamento<br>*O jah oonahltro ahppoontahmaynto* |
| I'm not very good at dancing/volleyball/swimming | Non so ballare/giocare a pallavolo/nuotare<br>*Non so bahllahray/jokahray ah pahllahvolo/nwotahray* |

## 3.9 Paying a compliment

| | |
|---|---|
| You look great! (formal/informal) | Sta/stai proprio bene!<br>*Stah/stahee propreeo bayhnay!* |
| I like your car! | Che bella macchina!<br>*Kay bayllah mahkkeenah!* |
| I like your ski outfit! | Che bel completo da sci!<br>*Kay bayl complayto dah shee!* |
| You are very nice (formal/informal) | È/sei molto gentile<br>*Ay/say molto jaynteelay* |
| What a good boy/girl! | Che bambino/a buono/a!<br>*Kay bahmbeeno/ah bwono/ah!* |
| You're (formal) a good dancer | (Lei) balla molto bene<br>*(Layee) bahllah molto bayhnay* |
| You're (formal) a very good cook | (Lei) cucina molto bene<br>*(Layee) koocheenah molto bayhnay* |
| You're (formal) a good footballer | (Lei) sa giocare molto bene a calcio<br>*(Layee) sah jokahray molto bayhnay ah kahlcheeo* |

## 3.10 Chatting someone up

| | |
|---|---|
| I like being with you | Mi piace stare con te<br>*Mee peeahchay stahray con tay* |
| I've missed you so much | Mi sei mancato/a tanto<br>*Mee say mahnkahto/ah tahnto* |
| I dreamt about you (m/f) | Ti ho sognato/a<br>*Tee o sonyahto/ah* |
| I think about you all day | Tutto il giorno penso a te<br>*Tootto eel jorno paynso ah tay* |
| I've been thinking about you all day | Ho pensato a te tutto il giorno<br>*O paynsahto ah tay tootto eel jorno* |
| You have such a sweet smile | Hai un bel sorriso<br>*Ahee oon bayl sorreezo* |
| You have such beautiful eyes | I tuoi occhi sono bellissimi<br>*Ee too-oee okkee sono baylleesseemee* |
| I love you (I'm fond of you) | Ti voglio bene<br>*Tee vollyo bayhnay* |
| I'm in love with you (m/f) | Sono innamorato/a di te<br>*Sono eennahmorahto/ah dee tay* |

| | |
|---|---|
| I'm in love with you too (m/f) | Anch'io sono innamorato/a di te<br>*Ankeeo sono eennahmorahto/ah dee tay* |
| I love you | Ti amo<br>*Tee ahmo* |
| I love you too | Anch'io ti amo<br>*Ahnkeeo tee ahmo* |
| I don't feel as strongly about you | I miei sentimenti verso di te non sono così intensi<br>*Ee meeay saynteemayntee vayrso dee tay non sono kozee eentaynsee* |
| I already have a girlfriend/boyfriend | Sono già fidanzato/a<br>*Sono jah feedahntzahto/ah* |
| I'm not ready for that | Me dispiace, non me la sento<br>*Mee deespeeahchay, non may lah saynto* |
| I don't want to rush into it | Non voglio precipitare le cose<br>*Non volleeo praycheepeetahray lay cosay* |
| Take your hands off me | Non toccarmi<br>*Non tokkahrmee* |
| Okay, no problem | O.k., non c'è problema<br>*O.K., non chay problaymah* |
| Will you spend the night with me? | Rimani con me stanotte?<br>*Reemahnee con may stahnottay?* |
| I'd like to go to bed with you | Vorrei andare a letto con te<br>*Vorrayee ahndahray ah laytto con tay* |
| Only if we use a condom | Soltanto con un preservativo<br>*Solo kon oon praysayrvahteevo* |
| We have to be careful about AIDS | Dobbiamo stare attenti a causa dell'aids<br>*Dobbyahmo stahray ahttayntee ah kaoosah dayll aheèids* |
| That's what they all say | Questo lo dicono tutti<br>*Kwaysto lo deekono toottee* |
| We shouldn't take any risks | Non possiamo correre rischi<br>*Non posseeahmo korrayray reeskee* |
| Do you have a condom? | Hai un preservativo?<br>*Ahee oon praysayrvahteevo?* |
| No? Then the answer's no | No? Allora lasciamo perdere<br>*No? Ahllorah lahshyahmo payrdayray* |

## 3.11 Arrangements

| | |
|---|---|
| When will I see you again? | Quando La/ti rivedrò?<br>*Kwahndo lah/tee reevaydro?* |
| Are you (informal) free over the weekend? | Sei libero/a al fine-settimana?<br>*Say leebayro/ah ahl feenay saytteemahnah?* |
| What's the plan, then? | Come rimaniamo d'accordo?<br>*Komay reemahnyahmo dahkkordo?* |
| Where shall we meet? | Dove ci vediamo?<br>*Dovay chee vaydyahmo?* |
| Will you pick me/us up? | Mi/ci verrà a prendere?<br>*Mee/chee vayrrah ah prayndayray?* |
| Shall I pick you (formal) up? | La passo a prendere?<br>*Lah pahsso ah prayndayray?* |
| I have to be home by... | Devo essere a casa alle...<br>*Dayvo ayssayray ah cahsah ahllay...* |
| I don't want to see you (formal) anymore | Non voglio più rivederLa<br>*Non volleeo peeoo reevaydayrlah* |

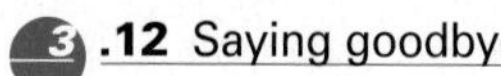

## 3.12 Saying goodbye

| | |
|---|---|
| Can I take you (formal) home? | Posso accompagnarLa a casa?<br>*Posso ahkkompahneeahrlah ah kahsah?* |
| Can I write/call you (formal)? | Posso scriverLe/chiamarLa?<br>*Posso skreevayrlay/keeahmahrlah?* |
| Will you (formal) write to me/call me? | Lei mi scriverà/chiamerà?<br>*Layeeh mee skreeverrah/keeahmaheerah?* |
| Can I have your address/phone number? | Mi dà il Suo indirizzo/numero di telefono?<br>*Mee dah eel sooo eendeereetzo/ noomayro dee taylayfono?* |
| Thanks for everything | Grazie di tutto<br>*Grahtzeeay dee tootto* |
| It was a lot of fun | E' stato molto divertente<br>*Ay stahto molto deevayrtayntay* |
| Say hello to (informal)... | Salutami...<br>*Sahlootahmee...* |
| All the best | Tante belle cose<br>*Tahntay bayllay kosay* |
| Good luck | Auguri<br>*Owgooree* |
| When will you (informal) be back? | Quando tornerai?<br>*Kwahndo tornayrahee?* |
| I'll be waiting for you (informal) | Ti aspetterò<br>*Tee ahspayttayrro* |
| I'd like to see you again | Vorrei rivederti<br>*Vorrayee reevaydayrtee* |
| I hope we meet again soon | Spero che ci rivedremo presto<br>*Spayro kay chee reevaydraymo praysto* |
| Here's our address. If you're ever in England... (formal) | Ecco il nostro indirizzo. Casomai venisse in Inghilterra...<br>*Aykko eel nostro eendeereetzo. Kahzomahee vayneessay een Eengeelltayrrah* |
| You'd be more than welcome (formal) | Saremo lieti di ospitarLa<br>*Sahrraymo leeaytee dee ospeetarlah* |

3 Conversation

# Eating out

# 4 Eating out



● **Eating establishments:**
*Trattoria*: middle-price restaurant
*Ristorante*: prices vary but with better service than a *Trattoria*
*Tavola calda*: cheap, self-service style
*Rosticceria*: large selection of mainly take-away meals
*Pizzeria*: specialising in pizza
*Osteria*: small trattoria or wine bar
*Gelateria*: specialising in icecream
*Bar/Caffè*: café also serving alcohol and snack food
*Birreria*: bar specialising in beer

● **Mealtimes:**
In Italy people usually have three meals:
1 *(Prima) colazione* (breakfast), is eaten sometime between 7.30 and 10 a.m., often standing up in a bar. It generally consists of *caffelatte* (white coffee) and biscuits or *cappuccino* with a *brioche* (croissant).
2 *Pranzo* (lunch), traditionally eaten at home between 1 and 2.30 p.m., includes a hot dish and is considered to be the most important meal of the day. Offices and shops often close and, unless enroled in a special afternoon programme, school children generally return home at lunchtime. Lunch usually consists of three courses:
- pasta or risotto
- main course of meat or fish with a vegetable or salad
- cheese and/or fruit

*Antipasti* (hors d'oeuvres preceding the pasta course), cakes and desserts are usually eaten on Sundays or on special occasions.
3 *Cena* (dinner), at around 8 or 9 p.m., is a light meal, often including soup, usually taken with the family.
At around 5 p.m., *merenda* (a snack) is often served to children and consists of bread and cured meats and/or cake.

● **In restaurants:** Most trattorias and restaurants have a cover charge (*coperto*) which includes bread, and a service charge.

## 4.1 On arrival

| | |
|---|---|
| I'd like to book a table for seven o'clock, please | Vorrei prenotare un tavolo per le sette?<br>*Vorrayee praynotahray oon tahvolo payr lay sayttay?* |
| A table for two, please | Un tavolo per due, per favore<br>*Oon tahvolo payr dooay payr fahvoray* |
| We've (We haven't) booked | (Non) abbiamo prenotato<br>*(Non) ahbbeeamo praynotahto* |

| | |
|---|---|
| Ha prenotato? | Do you have a reservation? |
| A che nome? | What name, please? |
| Prego, da questa parte | This way, please |
| Questo tavolo è prenotato | This table is reserved |
| Fra un quarto d'ora ci sarà un tavolo libero | We'll have a table free in fifteen minutes. |
| Le dispiace aspettare nel frattempo? | Would you mind waiting? |

| | |
|---|---|
| Is the restaurant open yet? | Il ristorante è già aperto?<br>*Eel reestorahntay ay jah ahpayrto?* |
| What time does the restaurant open?/What time does the restaurant close? | A che ora apre il ristorante/A che ora chiude il ristorante?<br>*Ah kay orah ahpray eel reestorahntay?/Ah kay orah keeooday eel reestorahntay?* |
| Can we wait for a table? | Possiamo aspettare che si liberi un tavolo?<br>*Possyahmo ahspayttahray kay see leebayree oon tahvolo?* |
| Do we have to wait long? | Dobbiamo aspettare parecchio?<br>*Dobbyahmo ahspayttahray pahraykkeeo?* |
| Is this seat taken? | E' libero questo posto?<br>*Ay leebayro kwaysto posto?* |
| Could we sit here/there? | Possiamo accomodarci qui/lì?<br>*Possyahmo ahkkomodahrchee kwee/lee?* |
| Can we sit by the window? | Possiamo sedere vicino alla finestra?<br>*Possyahmo sayhdayray veecheeno ahllah feenaystrah?* |
| Are there any tables outside? | Si può mangiare anche fuori?<br>*See pwo mahnjahray ahnkay fworee?* |
| Do you have another chair for us? | Ha un'altra sedia?<br>*Ah oonahltrah saydyah?* |
| Do you have a highchair? | Ha un seggiolone (per bambini)?<br>*Ah oon saydjolonay (payr bahmbeenee)?* |
| Is there a socket for this bottle-warmer? | C'è una presa di corrente per lo scaldabiberon?<br>*Chay oonah praysah dee corrayntay payr lo skahldahbeebayron?* |
| Could you warm up this bottle/jar for me? (in the microwave) | Potrebbe riscaldare questo biberon/vasetto (nel forno a microonde)?<br>*Potraybbay reeskahldahray kwaysto beebayron/vahzaytto (nayl forno ah meekro-onday)?* |
| Not too hot, please | Non bollente, per favore<br>*Non bollayntay payr fahvoray* |
| Is there somewhere I can change the baby's nappy? | C'è un posto dove posso cambiare il bambino/la bambina?<br>*Chay oon posto dovay posso kahmbeeahray eel bahmbeeno/lah bahmbeenah?* |
| Where are the toilets? | Dove è il bagno?<br>*Dovay ay eel bahnyo?* |

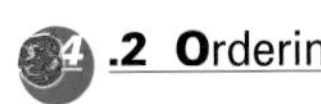

## 4.2 Ordering

| | |
|---|---|
| Waiter/Waitress! | Cameriere/a!<br>*Kahmayreeayray/ah!* |
| Madam! | Signora!<br>*Seeneeorah!* |
| Sir! | Signore!<br>*Seeneeoray!* |
| We'd like something to eat/drink | Vorremmo mangiare/bere qualcosa<br>*Vorraymmo mahnjahray/bayhray kwahlkosah* |
| Could I have a quick meal? | Potrei mangiare qualcosa rapidamente?<br>*Potray mahnjahray kwahlkosah rahpeedahmayntay?* |

|  |  |
|---|---|
| We don't have much time | Abbiamo poco tempo<br>*Ahbbeeahmo poko taympo* |
| We'd like to have a drink first | Vorremmo prima bere qualcosa<br>*Vorraymmo preemah bayhray kwahlkosah* |
| Could we see the menu/wine list, please? | Ci porta il menù/la lista dei vini, per favore?<br>*Chee portah eel maynoo/lah leestah dayee veenee payr fahvoray?* |
| Do you have a menu in English? | Ha un menù in inglese?<br>*Ah oon maynoo een eenglaysay?* |
| Do you have a dish of the day/a tourist menu? | Ha un piatto del giorno/un menù turistico?<br>*Ah oon peeahtto dayl jorno/oon maynoo tooreesteeko?* |
| We haven't made a choice yet. | Non abbiamo ancora deciso<br>*Non ahbbeeahmo ahnkorah daycheezo* |
| What do you recommend? | Cosa ci consiglia?<br>*Kosah chee konseellyah?* |
| What are the local specialities/your specialities? | Quali sono le specialità di questa regione/della casa?<br>*Kwahlee sono lay spaycheeahleetah dee kwaystah rayjonay/dayllah kahsah?* |
| I like strawberries/olives | Mi piacciono le fragole/le olive<br>*Mee peeahtchono lay frahgolay/lay oleevay* |
| I don't like meat/fish... | Non mi piace il pesce/la carne<br>*Non mee peeahchay eel payshay/lah kahrnay* |
| What's this? | Cosa è questo?<br>*Kosah ay kwaysto?* |
| Does it have...in it? | Contiene...?<br>*Konteeayhnay...?* |
| Is it stuffed with...? | E' farcito di...?<br>*Ay fahrcheeto dee...?* |
| What does it taste like? | Che sapore ha?<br>*Kay sahporay ah?* |
| Is this a hot or a cold dish? | E' un piatto caldo o freddo?<br>*Ay oon peeahtto kahldo o frayddo?* |
| Is this sweet? | E' dolce?<br>*Ay dolchay?* |
| Is this hot/spicy? | E' un piatto piccante/aromatizzato?<br>*Ay oon peeahtto peekkahntay/ ahromahteedzahto?* |

|  |  |
|---|---|
| Desidera? | What would you like? |
| Ha scelto? | Have you decided? |
| Vuole un aperitivo? | Would you like a drink first? |
| Cosa prende da bere? | What would you like to drink? |
| ... sono finiti/e | We've run out of..... |
| Buon appetito | Enjoy your meal/Bon appetit |
| Tutto bene? | Is everything all right? |
| Posso sparecchiare? | May I clear the table? |

| | |
|---|---|
| Do you have anything else, by any chance? | Avrebbe magari qualcos'altro?<br>*Ahvraybbay mahgahree kwahlkosahltro?* |
| I'm on a salt-free diet | Non posso mangiare sale<br>*Non posso mahnjahray sahlay* |
| I can't eat pork | Non posso mangiare carne di maiale<br>*Non posso mahnjahray kahrnay dee maheeahlay* |
| I can't have sugar | Non posso mangiare zuccheri<br>*Non posso mahnjahray dzookkayree* |
| I'm on a fat-free diet | Non posso mangiare grassi<br>*Non posso mahnjahray grahssee* |
| I can't have spicy food | Non posso mangiare cibi piccanti<br>*Non posso mahnjahray cheebee peekkahntee* |
| We'll have what those people are having | Vorremmo un piatto uguale al loro<br>*Vorraymmo oon peeahtto oogwahlay ahl loro* |
| I'd like... | Vorrei...<br>*Vorrayee...* |
| We're not having antipasto/a pasta dish | Passiamo subito al primo/secondo piatto<br>*Pahsseeahmo soobeeto ahl preemo/ saykondo peeahtto* |
| Could I have some more bread, please? | Mi porta un altro po' di pane, per favore?<br>*Mee portah oonahltro po dee pahnay payr fahvoray?* |
| Could I have another bottle of water/wine, please? | Mi porta un'altra bottiglia di acqua/di vino, per favore?<br>*Mee portah oonahltrah botteelleeah dee ahkwah/dee veeno payr fahvoray?* |
| Could I have another portion of...please? | Mi porta un'altra porzione di..., per favore?<br>*Mee portah oonahltrah portzeeonay dee..., payr fahvoray?* |
| Could I have the salt and pepper, please? | Mi porta il sale e il pepe, per favore?<br>*Mee portah eel sahlay ay eel paypay, payr fahvoray?* |
| Could I have a napkin, please? | Mi porta un tovagliolo, per favore?<br>*Mee portah oon tovallyolo, payr fahvoray?* |
| Could I have a teaspoon, please? | Mi porta un cucchiaino, per favore?<br>*Mee portah oon kookkeeaheeno payr fahvoray?* |
| Could I have an ashtray, please? | Mi porta un portacenere, per favore?<br>*Mee portah oon portahchaynayray, payr fahvoray?* |
| Could I have some matches, please? | Mi porta dei fiammiferi, per favore?<br>*Mee portah dayee feeahmmeefayree payr fahvoray?* |
| Could I have some toothpicks, please | Mi porta degli stuzzicadenti, per favore?<br>*Mee portah daylly stootzeekahdayntee payr fahvoray?* |
| Could I have a glass of water, please? | Mi porta un bicchiere d'acqua, per favore?<br>*Mee portah oon beekkeeayray dahkwah payr fahvoray?* |
| Could I have a straw please? | Mi porta una cannuccia, per favore?<br>*Mee portah oonah kahnnootchah payr fahvoray?* |
| Enjoy your meal/Bon appetit! | Buon appetito!<br>*Bwon ahppayteeto!* |

You too! ______ Grazie, altrettanto!
*Grahtzeeay, ahltrayttahnto!*

Cheers! ______ Cin cin!
*Cheen cheen!*

The next round's on me ______ La prossima volta offro io
*Lah prosseemah voltah offro eeo*

Could we have a doggy bag, please? ______ Potremmo portare via gli avanzi per il nostro cane?
*Potraymmo portahray veeah lly ahvahntzee payr eel nostro kahnay?*



##  .3 The bill

***See also 8.2 Settling the bill***

How much is this dish? ______ Quanto costa questo piatto?
*Kwahnto kostah kwaysto peeahtto?*

Could I have the bill, please? ______ Ci porti il conto
*Chee portee eel konto*

All together ______ Tutto insieme
*Tootto eensee-aymay*

Everyone pays separately/ let's go Dutch ______ Facciamo alla romana
*Fahtcheeahmo ahllah romahnah*

Could we have the menu again, please? ______ Ci porta di nuovo il menu?
*Chee portah dee nwovo eel maynoo?*

The...is not on the bill ______ Ha dimenticato di mettere il/la... sul conto
*Ah deemaynteekahto dee mayttayray eel/lah...sool konto*

##  .4 Complaints

It's taking a very long time ______ C'è ancora molto da aspettare?
*Chay ahnkorah molto dah ahspayttahray?*

We've been here an hour already ______ E' un'ora che stiamo qui
*Ay oonorah kay steeahmo kwee*

This must be a mistake ______ Senz'altro è uno sbaglio
*Saynzahltro ay oono sbahleeo*

This is not what I ordered ______ Non ho ordinato questo piatto
*Non o ordeenahto kwaysto peeahtto*

I ordered... ______ Ho chiesto...
*O keeaysto...*

There's a dish missing ______ Manca un piatto
*Mahnkah oon peeahtto*

This is broken/not clean ______ Questo è rotto/non è pulito
*Kwaysto ay rotto/non ay pooleeto*

The food's cold ______ Il piatto è freddo
*Eel peeahtto ay frayddo*

The food's not fresh ______ Il cibo non è fresco
*Eel cheebo non ay fraysko*

The food's too salty/ sweet/spicy ______ Il piatto è troppo salato/dolce/ aromatizzato
*Eel peeahtto ay troppo sahlahto/dolchay/ahromahteedzahto*

The meat's too rare ______ La carne è poco cotta
*Lah kahrnay ay poko kottah*

| | |
|---|---|
| The meat's overdone | La carne è troppo cotta<br>*Lah kahrnay ay troppo kottah* |
| The meat's tough | La carne è dura<br>*Lah kahrnay ay doorah* |
| The meat is off/has gone bad | La carne è andata a male<br>*Lah kahrnay ay ahndahtah ah mahlay* |
| Could I have something else instead of this? | Invece di questo, mi potrebbe dare un'altra cosa?<br>*Eenvayhchay dee kwaysto mee potraybbay dahray oonahltrah kosah?* |
| The bill/this amount is not right | Il conto non torna<br>*Eel konto non tornah* |
| We didn't have this | Non abbiamo preso questo<br>*Non ahbbeeahmo prayso kwaysto* |
| There's no paper in the toilet | Manca la carta igienica nel bagno<br>*Mahnkah lah kahrtah eejayneekah nayl bahneeo* |
| Will you call the manager, please? | Mi chiama il capo-servizio, per favore?<br>*Mee keeahmah eel kahpo-sayrveetzeeo payr fahvoray?* |

## 4.5 Paying a compliment

| | |
|---|---|
| That was a wonderful meal | Abbiamo mangiato molto bene<br>*Ahbbeeahmo mahnjahto molto bayhnay* |
| The food was excellent | Il cibo era ottimo<br>*Eel cheebo ayrah otteemo* |
| The...in particular was delicious | Soprattutto... era squisito/a<br>*Soprahttootto...ayrah skweezeeto/ah* |

## 4.6 The menu

antipasti
**starter/hors d'oeuvres**
cacciagione
**game**
carne
**meat**
contorni
**side dishes/vegetables**
coperto
**cover charge**
digestivo
**liqueur (after dinner)**
dolci
**cakes/desserts**
formaggio
**cheese**
frutta
**fruit**
gelati
**icecream**
insalata
**salad**
I.V.A.
**VAT**
minestra
**soup**
pane
**bread**
pasta(sciutta)
**pasta**
pesce
**fish**
pizza
**pizza**
pollame
**fowl**
primo piatto
**first course**
secondo piatto
**main course**
servizio (compreso)
**service charge (included)**
specialità
**specialities**
spuntini
**snacks**
verdure
**vegetables**

## 4.7 Alphabetical list of drinks and dishes

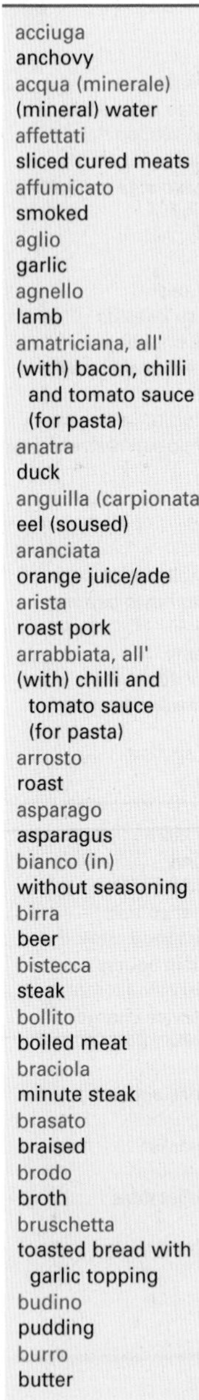

acciuga
anchovy

acqua (minerale)
(mineral) water

affettati
sliced cured meats

affumicato
smoked

aglio
garlic

agnello
lamb

amatriciana, all'
(with) bacon, chilli and tomato sauce (for pasta)

anatra
duck

anguilla (carpionata)
eel (soused)

aranciata
orange juice/ade

arista
roast pork

arrabbiata, all'
(with) chilli and tomato sauce (for pasta)

arrosto
roast

asparago
asparagus

bianco (in)
without seasoning

birra
beer

bistecca
steak

bollito
boiled meat

braciola
minute steak

brasato
braised

brodo
broth

bruschetta
toasted bread with garlic topping

budino
pudding

burro
butter

cacciatora, alla
(with) mushroom sauce (esp. for chicken)

caffè corretto/macchiato
laced or flavoured coffee/coffee with a drop of milk

caffè freddo
iced coffee

caffè (lungo/ristretto)
coffee (weak/strong)

caffellatte
Café au lait/milky coffee

calamaro
squid

cannelloni
cannelloni (pasta tubes)

cappero
caper

cappuccino
cappuccino (coffee with frothy milk)

carbonara, alla
(with) cream, bacon, egg, black pepper and parmesan sauce (for pasta)

carciofo
artichoke

carota
carrot

carpa
carp

carrettiera, alla
(with) tomato, garlic, chilli and parsley sauce (for pasta)

casalingo
home-made

cassata
cassata (Sicilian fruited icecream)

cavolfiore
cauliflower

cavolini di Bruxelles
Brussels sprouts

cavolo
cabbage

ceci
chick peas

cervello
brains

cervo
venison

cetriolino
gherkin

cetriolo
cucumber

cicoria
chicory

cinghiale
boar

cioccolata
chocolate

cipolla
onion

coda di bue
oxtail

condito
dressed

coniglio
rabbit

coscia
leg (of chicken, of lamb)

cotoletta
cutlet

cozze
mussels

crema
custard

crostini
canapé with savoury topping/croutons

crudo
raw

digestivo
liqueur (after dinner)

erbe aromatiche
herbs

fagiano
pheasant

fagioli
beans

fagiolini
green beans

faraona
guinea fowl

farcito
stuffed

fegato
liver
alla brace
barbequed/grilled
fetta/fettina
slice/thin slice
filetto
fillet
finocchio
fennel
forno, al
baked
frappé
milk-shake
frittata
omelette
fritto
fried
frizzante
fizzy
frullato
milk-shake/whisked
frutti di mare
seafood
funghi
mushrooms
gamberetto
shrimp
gambero
crayfish
gelato
icecream
ghiaccio (con)
(with) ice
giardiniera, alla
(with) vegetable sauce
gnocchi
potato dumplings
granchio
crab
gran(o)turco
corn
grappa
eau de vie
griglia, alla
grilled
imbottito
stuffed
infuso
infusion (tea)
intingolo di lepre
hare sauce
involtino
roulade
latte
milk
lepre
hare
limone (al)
(with) lemon
lingua
tongue
liquore
liqueur
lombata/lombo
loin
luccio
pike
lumache
snails
maccheroni
macaroni (pasta)
macedonia di frutta
fruit salad
manzo
beef
marinato
marinated/pickled
melanzana
eggplant/aubergine
merluzzo
cod
miele
honey
minestrone
minestrone soup
molluschi
shellfish
noce
walnut
noce moscata
nutmeg
olio
oil
oliva
olive
ossobuco
veal shin
ostrica
oyster
pancetta
bacon
pane (integrale/tostato)
bread (wholemeal/ toasted)
panino (imbottito)
bread-roll (filled)
panna (montata)
(whipped) cream
parmigiano
parmesan (cheese)
passata
sieved or creamed
pasta
pasta
pastasciutta
pasta (with sauce)
pasta sfoglia
puff pastry
pasticcio
(sort of) pie (often made of pasta)
patate fritte
chips
pecora
sheep/mutton
pecorino
sheep's milk cheese
penne
pasta quills
peperoncino
chilli
peperone
(green, red, yellow) pepper
pesto
basil,pine-nut and parmesan sauce
petto
breast
piccione
pigeon
piselli
peas
pizzaiola, alla
(with) mozzarella cheese, oregano and tomato sauce
pollo
chicken
polpetta
meatball
pomodoro
tomato
porchetta
suckling pig
porcini
(porcini) mushrooms
porto
Port (wine)
prezzemolo
parsley
prosciutto
cured ham
puttanesca, alla
(with) spicy tomato sauce

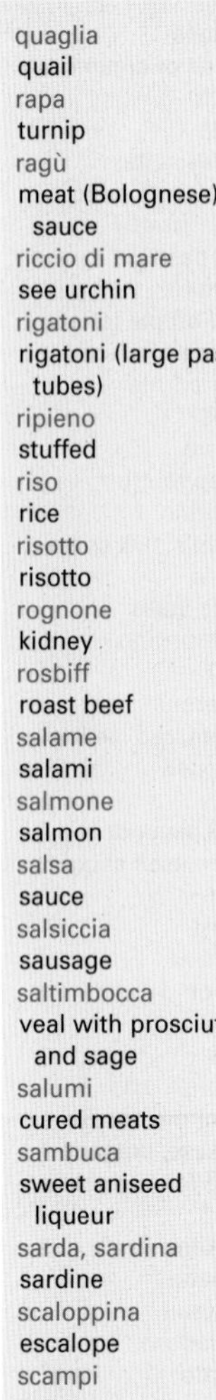



quaglia
quail

rapa
turnip

ragù
meat (Bolognese) sauce

riccio di mare
see urchin

rigatoni
rigatoni (large pasta tubes)

ripieno
stuffed

riso
rice

risotto
risotto

rognone
kidney

rosbiff
roast beef

salame
salami

salmone
salmon

salsa
sauce

salsiccia
sausage

saltimbocca
veal with prosciutto and sage

salumi
cured meats

sambuca
sweet aniseed liqueur

sarda, sardina
sardine

scaloppina
escalope

scampi
prawns

secco
dry

sedano
celery

sel(t)z
soda water

selvaggina
game

semifreddo
icecream cake

senape
mustard

seppia
cuttle fish

sogliola
sole

sottaceti
pickles

spalla
shoulder

spezzatino
stew

spiedo, allo
on the spit

spina, alla
draught (beer)

spinaci
spinach

spremuta
(freshly squeezed) juice

spumante
sparkling wine

S.Q. secondo quantità
according to weight

stracciatella
soup: broth with beaten egg

stufato
stew

succo di frutta
fruit juice

sugo
sauce

tacchino
turkey

tagliatelle
tagliatelle (flat ribbon pasta)

tartaruga
turtle

tartufo
truffle

tè
tea

testa (di vitello)
head (of veal)

tonno
tuna

torta
pie/cake

tortellini
tortellini (kind of stuffed pasta)

trippa
tripe

trita(ta)
minced or ground (usually herbs or meat)

trota
trout

uova strapazzate
scrambled eggs

uovo affogato/in camicia
poached egg

uovo al tegame/fritto
fried egg

uovo, all'
(with) egg

uovo alla coque/da bere/sodo
soft boiled/fresh/hard boiled egg

vaniglia
vanilla

verdura
green vegetables

vino bianco/rosso/rosato
white/red/rosé wine

vitello
veal

vongola
clam

zabaione
zabaglione (sweet custard sauce made with egg and Marsala)

zucchero
sugar

zucchino
courgette (small marrow, squash)

zuppa
soup

zuppa alla pavese
kind of broth

zuppa inglese
kind of trifle

# On the road

# 5 On the road

## 5.1 Asking for directions

| | |
|---|---|
| Excuse me, could I ask you something? | Mi scusi, potrei chiederLe una cosa?<br>*Mee skoozee potray keeaydayrlay oonah kozah?* |
| I've lost my way | Mi sono perso/a<br>*Mee sono payrso/ah* |
| Is there a(n)... around here? | Sa se c'è un/una...da queste parti?<br>*Sah say chay oon/oonah...dah kwaystay pahrtee?* |
| Is this the way to...? | E' questa la strada per...?<br>*Ay kwaystah lah strahdah payr...* |
| Could you tell me how to get to....? | Mi può indicare la strada per...?<br>*Mee pwo eendeekahray lah strahdah payr...* |
| What's the quickest way to...? | Qual'è la strada più diretta per...?<br>*Kwahlay ay lah strahdah peeoo deerayttah payr...?* |
| How many kilometres is it to...? | A quanti chilometri è...?<br>*Ah qwahntee keelomaytreeay....?* |
| Could you point it out on the map? | Me lo può indicare sulla mappa?<br>*May lo pwo eendeekahray soollah mahppah?* |



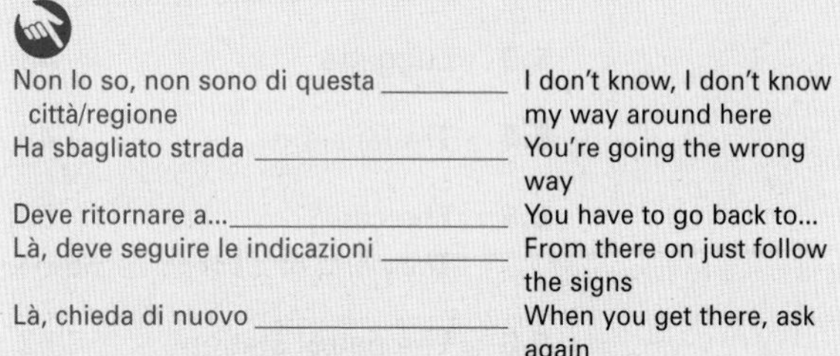

| | |
|---|---|
| Non lo so, non sono di questa città/regione | I don't know, I don't know my way around here |
| Ha sbagliato strada | You're going the wrong way |
| Deve ritornare a... | You have to go back to... |
| Là, deve seguire le indicazioni | From there on just follow the signs |
| Là, chieda di nuovo | When you get there, ask again |

Vada dritto
Go straight ahead
Giri a sinistra
Turn left
Giri a destra
Turn right
Volti a destra/sinistra
Turn right/left
Segua
Follow
Attraversi
Cross
l'incrocio
the intersection/crossroads

la strada
the road/street
il semaforo
the traffic light
la galleria
the tunnel
il cartello/segnale stradale di 'dare la precedenza'
the "give way" sign
il palazzo
the building
all'angolo
at the corner

il fiume
the river
il viadotto
the flyover
il ponte
the bridge
il passaggio a livello
the level crossing
le indicazioni per...
the signs pointing to....
la freccia
the arrow

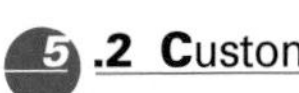

## 5.2 Customs

By law you must always carry with you an identification document and, if driving, your driving licence.

- **Border documents:** valid passport. Citizens of EU countries may enter Italy using a national identity card. Strictly speaking, visitors planning to stay at the same address for more than one week need a *permesso di soggiorno*, obtained from the *questura* (police station) and requiring a visa stamp. This only becomes a necessity if you plan to study, work or live in Italy.
- **For car and motorbike:** valid driving licence (non-EU licences require an Italian translation or an International Driving Permit); vehicle registration document; third party international insurance document (Green Card).
- **Caravan:** same registration numberplate and Green Card.

A warning triangle is compulsory (bulb kit, fire extinguisher and first-aid kit are recommended).

- **Import and export specifications:**

| | |
|---|---|
| – Foreign currrency: | no restrictions on the import of lire. |
| – Alcohol: | 1 lt spirits or liquor, 2 lts wine or fortified wine. |
| – Tobacco: | 200 cigarettes, 50 cigars, 250g tobacco |
| – Perfume: | 50g perfume, 250ml eau de toilette |
| – Coffee: | 500g |
| – Tea: | 100g |

You must be aged 17 to import alcohol and tobacco and 15 to import coffee and tea. The above restrictions are relevant to all alcohol and tobacco purchased in duty-free shops and will apply until 30/6/99.

| | |
|---|---|
| Il passaporto, prego | Your passport, please |
| La carta verde, prego | Your green card, please |
| Il libretto d'immatricolazione, prego | Your vehicle documents, please |
| Il visto, prego | Your visa, please |
| Dove va? | Where are you going? |
| Quanto tempo intende rimanere? | How long are you planning to stay? |
| Ha qualcosa da dichiarare? | Do you have anything to declare? |
| Per favore, mi apra questo/a | Open this, please |

| | |
|---|---|
| My children are entered on this passport | I miei figli sono su questo passaporto<br>*Ee meeayee feelly sono soo kwaysto pahssahporto* |
| I'm travelling through | Sono di passaggio<br>*Sono dee pahssahdjo* |
| I'm going on holiday to... | Passerò le vacanze a...<br>*Pahssayhro lay vahkahntzay ah...* |
| I'm on a business trip | Sono in viaggio d'affari<br>*Sono een veeahdjo dahffahree* |
| I don't know how long I'll be staying | Non so quanto tempo rimarrò<br>*Non so kwahnto taympo reemahrro* |
| I'll be staying here for a weekend | Rimarrò qui un weekend<br>*Reemahrro kwee oon weekend* |
| I'll be staying here for a few days | Rimarrò qui qualche giorno<br>*Reemahrro kwee kwahlkay jorno* |

| | |
|---|---|
| I'll be staying here a week | Rimarrò qui una settimana<br>*Reemahrro kwee oonah saytteemahnah* |
| I'll be staying here for two weeks | Rimarrò qui due settimane<br>*Reemahrro kwee dooay saytteemahnay* |
| I've got nothing to declare | Non ho niente da dichiarare<br>*Non o neeayntay dah deekeeahrahray* |
| I have... | Ho...<br>*O...* |
| – a carton of cigarettes | – una stecca di sigarette<br>*– oonah staykkah dee seegahrayttay* |
| – a bottle of... | – una bottiglia di...<br>*– oonah botteellyah dee...* |
| – some souvenirs | – qualche souvenir<br>*– kwahlkay sovayneer* |
| These are personal effects | Sono oggetti personali<br>*Sono odjayttee payrsonahlee* |
| These are not new | Questa roba non è nuova<br>*Kwaystah robah non ay nwovah* |
| Here's the receipt | Ecco lo scontrino<br>*Aykko lo skontreeno* |
| This is for private use | E' per uso personale<br>*Ay payr oozo payrsonahlay* |
| How much import duty do I have to pay? | Quanto devo pagare di tassa d'importazione?<br>*Kwahnto dayvo pahgahray dee tahssah deemportahtzeeonay ?* |
| May I go now? | Posso andare adesso?<br>*Posso ahndahray ahdaysso?* |

## 5.3 Luggage

| | |
|---|---|
| Porter! | Facchino!<br>*Fahkkeeno!* |
| Could you take this luggage to...? | Per favore, potrebbe portare questi bagagli a...<br>*Payr fahvoray, potraybbay portahray kwaystee bahgahlly ah...* |
| How much do I owe you? | Quanto Le devo?<br>*Kwahnto lay dayvo?* |
| Where can I find a trolley? | Dove posso trovare un carrello?<br>*Dovay posso trovahray oon kahrrello?* |
| Could you store this luggage for me? | E' possibile lasciare in consegna questi bagagli?<br>*Ay posseebeelay lahsheeahray een konsayneeah kwaystee bahgahlly?* |
| Where are the luggage lockers? | Dove sono le cassette per la custodia dei bagagli?<br>*Dovay sono lay kahssayttay payr lah koostodeeah dayee bahgahlly?* |
| I can't get the locker open | Non riesco ad aprire la cassetta<br>*Non ree-aysko ahdahpreeray lah kahssaytta* |
| How much is it per item per day? | Quanto costa al giorno ogni collo?<br>*Kwahnto kostah ahl jorno onyee kollo?* |
| This is not my bag/ suitcase | Non è la mia borsa/valigia<br>*Non ay lah meeah borsah/vahleejah* |

| | |
|---|---|
| There's one item/bag/suitcase missing | Manca un collo/una borsa/una valigia<br>*Mahnkah oon kollo/oonah borsah/oonah vahleejah* |
| My suitcase is damaged | La mia valigia è danneggiata<br>*Lah meeah vahleejah ay dahnnaydjahtah* |

## 5.4 Traffic signs

|  |  |
|---|---|
| accendere i fari (in galleria) | switch on headlights (in the tunnel) |
| alt | stop |
| area/stazione di servizio | service station |
| attenzione | beware |
| autocarri | heavy goods vehicles |
| banchina non transitabile | impassable verge |
| caduta massi | beware, falling rocks |
| cambiare corsia | change lanes |
| chiuso al traffico | road closed |
| corsia di emergenza | emergency lane |
| curve | bends |
| deviazione | detour |
| disco orario (obbligatorio) | parking disk (compulsory) |
| divieto di accesso | no entry |
| divieto di sorpasso/di sosta | no overtaking/no parking |
| diritto di precedenza a fine strada | right of way at end of road |
| galleria | tunnel |
| incrocio | intersection/crossroads |
| (isola/zona) pedonale | traffic island/pedestrian precinct |
| lasciare libero il passo/passaggio | do not obstruct |
| lavori in corso | roadworks |
| pagamento/pedaggio | toll payment |
| parcheggio a pagamento/riservato a... | paying carpark/parking reserved for... |
| parcheggio custodito | supervised carpark |
| passaggio a livello | level crossing |
| altezza limitata a... | maximum head room... |
| passo carrabile | driveway |
| pericolo(so) | danger(ous) |
| pioggia o gelo per km.... | rain or ice for...kms |
| precedenza | right of way |
| rallentare | slow down |
| senso unico | one way |
| senso vietato | no entry |
| soccorso stradale | road assistance (breakdown service) |
| sosta limitata | parking for a limited period |
| strada deformata/in dissesto | broken/uneven surface |
| strada interrotta | road closed |
| strettoia | narrowing in the road |
| tenere la destra/sinistra | keep right/left |
| traffico interrotto | road blocked |
| transito con catene | snow-chains required |
| uscita | exit |
| velocità massima | maximum speed |
| vietato l'accesso/ai pedoni | no access/no pedestrian access |
| vietato l'autostop | no hitch-hiking |
| vietato svoltare a destra/sinistra | no right/left turn |
| zona disco | disk zone |
| zona rimozione (ambo i lati) | tow-away area (both sides of the road) |

## The parts of a car

(the diagram shows the numbered parts)

| | | | |
|---|---|---|---|
| 1 | battery | batteria | *bahttayreeyah* |
| 2 | rear light | il fanale posteriore | *eel fahnahlay postayryoray* |
| 3 | rear-view mirror | lo specchietto retrovisore | *lo spaykkeeaytto raytroveezoray* |
| | reversing light | la luce di retromarcia | *lah loochay dee raytromahrcheeah* |
| 4 | aerial | antenna | *ahntaynnah* |
| | car radio | autoradio (f) | *ahootorahdeeo* |
| 5 | petrol tank | serbatoio carburante | *sayrbahtoeeo kahrboorahntay* |
| 6 | sparking plugs | le candele | *lay kahndaylay* |
| | fuel pump | pompa della benzina | *pompah dayllah bayndzeenah* |
| 7 | wing mirror | lo specchietto retrovisore esterno | *lo spaykkeeaytto raytroveezoray aystayrno* |
| 8 | bumper | il paraurti | *eel pahrah-oortee* |
| | carburettor | il carburatore | *eel kahrboorahtoray* |
| | crankcase | basamento del motore | *bahsahmayhnto dayl motoray* |
| | cylinder | cilindro | *cheeleendro* |
| | ignition | accensione (f) | *ahtchaynseeonay* |
| | warning light | spia luminosa | *spee-ah loomeenohzah* |
| | dynamo | la dinamo | *lah deenahmo* |
| | accelerator | acceleratore (m) | *ahtchayllayrahtoray* |
| | handbrake | freno a mano | *frayno ah mahno* |
| | valve | valvola | *vahlvolah* |
| 9 | silencer | marmitta | *mahrmeettah* |
| 10 | boot | cofano | *kofahno* |
| 11 | headlight | faro | *fahro* |
| | crank shaft | albero a gomiti | *ahlbayro ah gomeetee* |
| 12 | air filter | filtro dell aria | *feeltro dayllahreea* |
| | fog lamp | faro fendinebbia | *fahro fayndeenaybbeeah* |
| 13 | engine block | monoblocco | *monoblokko* |
| | camshaft | albero a camme | *ahlbayro ah kahmmay* |
| | oil filter/pump | filtro/pompa dell'olio | *feeltro/pompah daylloleeo* |
| | dipstick | indicatore (m) di livello dell'olio | *eendeekahtoray dee leevayllo daylloleeo* |
| | pedal | il pedale | *eel paydahlay* |
| 14 | door | portiera | *porteeayrah* |
| 15 | radiator | il radiatore | *eel rahdeeahtoray* |
| 16 | brake disc | disco del freno | *deesko dayl frayno* |
| | spare wheel | ruota di scorta | *rwohtah dee skortah* |
| 17 | indicator | indicatore (m) (di direzione) | *eendeekahtoray (dee deeraytzeeonay)* |
| 18 | windscreen wiper | tergicristallo | *tayrjeekreestahllo* |
| 19 | shock absorbers | ammortizzatore (m) | *ahmmorteedzahtoray* |
| | sunroof | tetto apribile | *taytto ahpreebeelay* |
| | spoiler | lo spoiler | *lo spoeelayr* |
| | starter motor | motorino di avviamento | *motoreeno dee ahvveeahmaynto* |

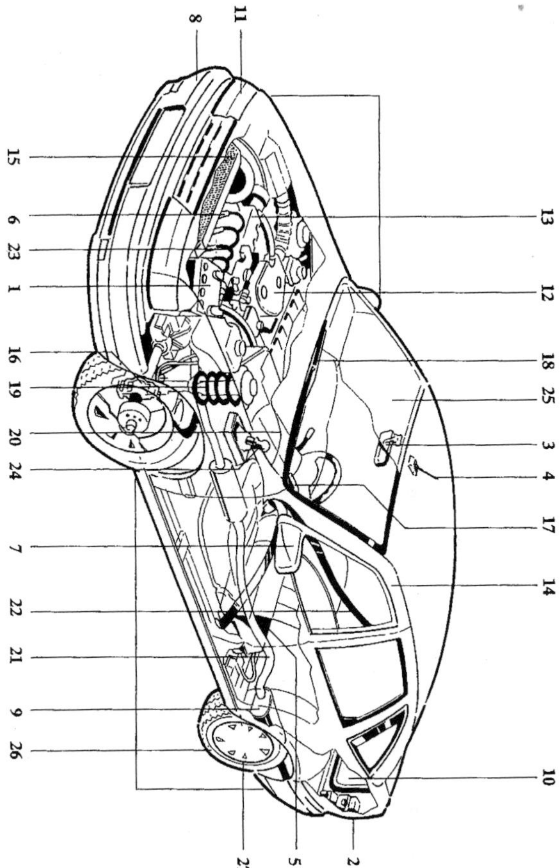


| | | |
|---|---|---|
| 20 steering column | il piantone dello sterzo | *eel peeahntonay dayllo stayrtzo* |
| steering wheel | il volante | *eel volahntay* |
| 21 exhaust pipe | tubo di scarico | *toobo dee skahreeko* |
| 22 seat belt | cintura di sicurezza | *cheentoorah dee seekooraytzah* |
| fan | il ventilatore | *eel vaynteelahtoray* |
| 23 distributor cables | i cavi del distributore | *ee kahvee dayl deestreebootoray* |
| 24 gear lever | leva del cambio | *layvah del kahmbeeo* |
| 25 windscreen | il parabrezza | *eel pahrahbrayzah* |
| water pump | pompa dell'acqua | *pompah dayllahkkwah* |
| 26 wheel | ruota | *rwotah* |
| 27 hubcap | coprimozzo | *kopreemotzo* |
| piston | il pistone | *eel peestonay* |

## 5.5 The car

*See the diagram on page 51.*

● **Particular traffic regulations:**
**Speed limits:** on *autostradas* 130 km/h for cars of 1100cc or more; 110km/h for smaller cars and motorbikes under 350cc.
On all main, non-urban highways 110 km/h; on secondary, non-urban highways 90 km/h; in built-up areas 50 km/h.
**Give way** to vehicles coming from the right unless otherwise indicated.
– towing: prohibited to private drivers.

## 5.6 The petrol station

● **The cost of petrol** in Italy is very high (around L. 1,500/litre), slightly less for unleaded.

| | |
|---|---|
| How many kilometres to the next petrol station, please? | A quanti chilometri sta il prossimo distributore di benzina?<br>*Ah kwahntee keelomaytree sta eel prossemo deestreebootoray dee baynzeenah?* |
| I would like...litres of | Vorrei...litri di<br>*Vorrayee...leetree dee* |
| – super | Vorrei...litri di super<br>*Vorrayee... leetree dee soopayr* |
| – leaded | Vorrei...litri di normale<br>*Vorrayee... leetree dee normahlay* |
| – unleaded | Vorrei...litri di benzina senza piombo<br>*Vorrayee...leetree dee baynzeenah saynzah peeombo* |
| – diesel | Vorrei...litri di gasolio<br>*Vorrayee... leetree dee gahzoleeo* |
| ... lire worth of gas | Vorrei...lire di benzina<br>*Vorrayee...leeray dee baynzeenah* |
| Fill her up, please | Mi faccia il pieno per favore<br>*Mee fahtchah eel peeayno payr fahvoray* |
| Could you check...? | Può controllarmi...?<br>*Pwo controllahrmee...?* |
| – the oil level | – il livello dell'olio<br>*– eel leevayllo daylloleeo* |
| – the tyre pressure | – la pressione delle gomme<br>*– lah praysseeonay dayllay gommay* |
| Could you change the oil, please? | Può cambiarmi l'olio?<br>*Pwo kahmbeeahrmeo loleeo?* |
| Could you clean the windscreen, please? | Può lavarmi il parabrezza?<br>*Pwo lahvahrmeo eel pahrahbraydzah?* |
| Could you give the car a wash, please? | Può lavarmi la macchina?<br>*Pwo lahvahrmee lah mahkkeenah?* |

## 5.7 Breakdown and repairs

| | |
|---|---|
| I have broken down Could you give me a hand? | Sono rimasto/a in panne. Mi potrebbe dare una mano?<br>*Sono reaymahsto/ah een pahnnay. Mee potraybbay dahray oonah mahno?* |

| | |
|---|---|
| I (m/f) have run out of petrol | Sono rimasto/a senza benzina<br>*Sono reaymahsto/ah saynzah bayndzeenah* |
| I've locked the keys in the car | Ho chiuso le chiavi in macchina<br>*O keeoozo lay keeahvee een mahkkeenah* |
| The car/motorbike/ moped won't start | La macchina/la moto (cicletta)/il motorino non parte<br>*Lah mahkkeenah/lah moto(cheeklayttah)/eel motoreeno non pahrtay* |
| Could you contact the breakdown service for me, please? | Può chiamarmi il soccorso stradale?<br>*Pwo keeahmahrmee eel sokkorso strahdahlay?* |
| Could you call a garage for me, please? | Può chiamarmi un garage?<br>*Pwo keeahmahrmee oon gahrahj?* |
| Could you give me a lift to...? | Mi darebbe un passaggio fino... ?<br>*Mee dahraybbay oon pahssahdjo feeno...?* |
| – to the nearest garage? | – al prossimo garage?<br>*– ahl prosseemo gahraj?* |
| – to the nearest town? | – fino alla prossima città?<br>*– feeno ahllah prosseemah cheettah?* |
| – to the nearest telephone booth? | – fino al prossimo telefono pubblico?<br>*– feeno ahl prosseemo taylayfono poobbleeko?* |
| – to the nearest emergency phone? | – fino al prossimo telefono di emergenza?<br>*– feeno ahl posseemo taylayfono dee aymayrjayntzah?* |
| Can we take my moped? | Può caricare il mio motorino?<br>*Pwo kahreekahray eel meeo motoreeno?* |
| Could you tow me to a garage? | Può trainarmi a un garage?<br>*Pwo traheenahrmee ah oon gahrahj?* |
| There's probably something wrong with...(See 5.5) | Probabilmente si è guastato/a/si sono guastati/e...<br>*Probahbeelmayntay see ay gwahstahto/ah see sono gwahstahtee/ay...* |
| Can you fix it? | Me lo potrebbe aggiustare?<br>*May lo potraybbay ahdjoostahray?* |
| Could you fix my tyre? | Mi potrebbe aggiustare la gomma?<br>*Mee potraybbay ahdjoostahray lah gommah?* |
| Could you change this wheel? | Potrebbe cambiare questa ruota?<br>*Potraybbay kahmbeeahray kwaystah rwotah?* |
| Can you fix it so it'll get me to...? | Me lo potrebbe aggiustare in modo da poter arrivare fino a...?<br>*May lo potraybbay ahdjoostahray een modo dah potayr ahrreevahray feeno ah...?* |
| Which garage can help me? | Quale altro garage potrebbe aiutarmi?<br>*Kwahlay ahltro gahrahj potraybbay aheeootahrmee?* |
| When will my car/ bicycle be ready? | La mia macchina/bicicletta, quando sarà pronta?<br>*Lah meeah mahkkeenah/beecheeklettah kwahndo sahrah prontah?* |
| Have you already finished? | Ha già finito?<br>*Hah djah feeneeto?* |
| Can I wait for it here? | Posso restare qui ad aspettare?<br>*Posso raystahray kwee ahdahspayttahray?* |
| How much will it cost? | Quanto verrà a costare?<br>*Kwahnto vayrrah ah costahray?* |

## The parts of a bicycle

(the diagram shows the numbered parts)

| |  |  |  |
|---|---|---|---|
| 1 | rear lamp | fanalino posteriore | *fahnahleeno postayreeoray* |
| 2 | rear wheel | ruota posteriore | *rwotah postayreeoray* |
| 3 | (luggage) carrier | il portapacchi | *eel portahpahkkee* |
| 4 | fork | forcella | *forchayllah* |
| 5 | bell | campanello | *kahmpahnayllo* |
| | inner tube | camera d'aria | *kahmayrah dahreeyah* |
| | tyre | gomma | *gommah* |
| 6 | peddle crank | pedivella | *payhdeevayllah* |
| 7 | gear change | cambio | *kahmbeeo* |
| | wire | filo | *feelo* |
| | dynamo | la dinamo | *lah deenahmo* |
| | bicycle trailer | carrello | *kahrrayllo* |
| | frame | telaio | *tayllahee-oh* |
| 8 | wheel guard | il pararuota | *eel pahrah-rwohtah* |
| 9 | chain | catena | *kahtaynah* |
| | chain guard | il copricatena | *eel kopreekahtaynah* |
| | odometer | il contachilometri | *eel kontahkeelomayhtree* |
| | child's seat | il seggiolino | *eel saydjholeeno* |
| 10 | headlamp | il fanale | *eel fahnahlay* |
| | bulb | lampadina | *lahmpahdeenah* |
| 11 | pedal | il pedale | *eel paydahlay* |
| 12 | pump | pompa | *pompah* |
| 13 | reflector | il catarifrangente | *eel kahtahreefrahndjayhntay* |
| 14 | brake pad | pastiglia | *pahsteelleeah* |
| 15 | brake cable | cavo del freno | *kahvo dayl frayno* |
| 16 | anti-theft device | antifurto (m) | *ahnteefoorto* |
| 17 | carrier straps | le cinghie del portapacchi | *lay cheengeeay dayl portahpahkkee* |
| | tachometer | tachimetro | *tahkeemaytro* |
| 18 | spoke | raggio | *rahjeeo* |
| 19 | mudguard | parafango | *pahrahfahngo* |
| 20 | handlebar | manubrio | *mahnoobreeo* |
| 21 | chain wheel | ruota dentata | *rwotah dayntahtah* |
| | toe clip | il fermapiede | *eel fayrmahpeeayday* |
| 22 | crank axle | albero delle pedivelle | *ahlbayro dayllay paydeevayllay* |
| | drum brake | freno a tamburo | *frayno ah tahmbooro* |
| 23 | rim | il cerchione | *eel chayrkeeonay* |
| 24 | valve | valvola | *vahlvolah* |
| 25 | gear cable | cavo del cambio | *kahvo dayl kahmbeeo* |
| 26 | fork | forcella | *forchayllah* |
| 27 | front wheel | ruota anteriore | *rwotah ahntayreeoray* |
| 28 | seat | sellino (sella) | *saylleeno (sayllah)* |

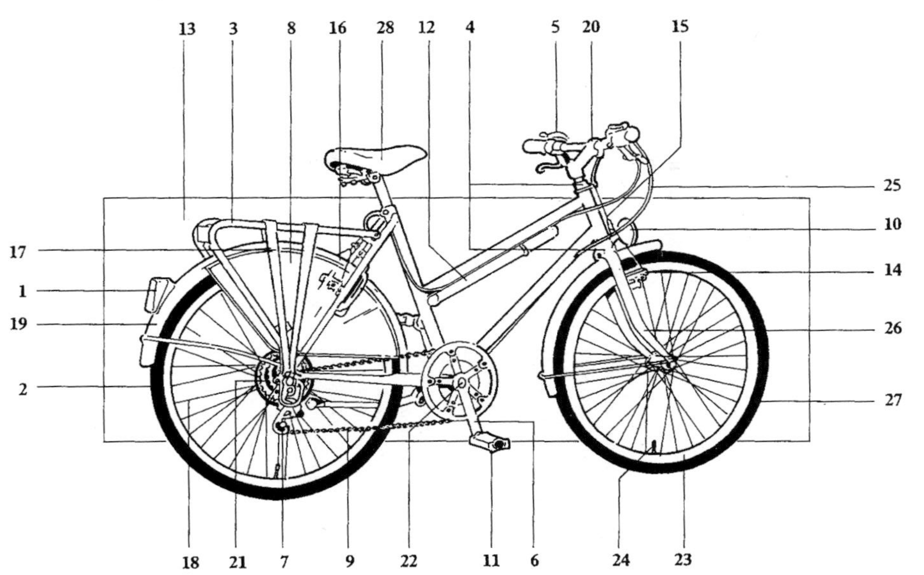
13
3
8
16
28
12
4
5
20
15
17
1
19
2
25
10
14
26
27
18
21
7
9
22
11
6
24
23

| | |
|---|---|
| Could you itemise the bill? | Mi potrebbe dettagliare il conto?<br>*Mee potraybbay dayttahllyahray eel konto?* |
| Could you give me a receipt for insurance purposes? | Mi potrebbe dare una ricevuta per l'assicurazione?<br>*Mee potraybbay dahray oonah reechayvootah payr lahsseekoorahtzeeonay?* |

## 5.8 The bicycle/moped

***See the diagram on page 55.***

● **Cycle paths** are rare in Italy. Bikes can be hired in most Italian towns. Not much consideration for bikes should be expected on the roads. The maximum speed for mopeds is 40 km/h but you should be aged 14 and over. A crash helmet is compulsory up to the age of 18, and a new law is being considered to make helmets compulsory for anyone. This should be checked when you arrive.



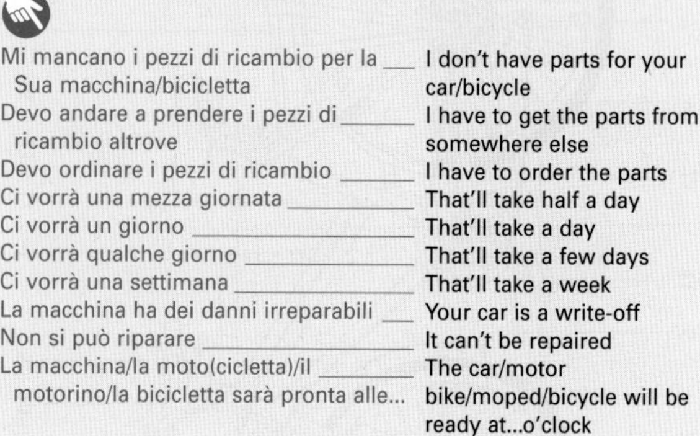

| | |
|---|---|
| Mi mancano i pezzi di ricambio per la Sua macchina/bicicletta | I don't have parts for your car/bicycle |
| Devo andare a prendere i pezzi di ricambio altrove | I have to get the parts from somewhere else |
| Devo ordinare i pezzi di ricambio | I have to order the parts |
| Ci vorrà una mezza giornata | That'll take half a day |
| Ci vorrà un giorno | That'll take a day |
| Ci vorrà qualche giorno | That'll take a few days |
| Ci vorrà una settimana | That'll take a week |
| La macchina ha dei danni irreparabili | Your car is a write-off |
| Non si può riparare | It can't be repaired |
| La macchina/la moto(cicletta)/il motorino/la bicicletta sarà pronta alle... | The car/motor bike/moped/bicycle will be ready at...o'clock |

## 5.9 Renting a vehicle

| | |
|---|---|
| I'd like to rent a... | Vorrei noleggiare un/una...<br>*Vorray nolaydgeeahray oon/oonah...* |
| Do I need a (special) licence for that? | Mi occorre una patente speciale?<br>*Mee okkorray oonah pahtayntay spaych-eeahlay?* |
| I'd like to rent the...for... | Vorrei noleggiare il/la... per...<br>*Vorrayee nolaydgeeahray eel/lah...payr...* |
| the...for a day | il/la...per un giorno<br>*eel/lah...payr oon jorno* |
| the...for two days | il/la...per due giorni<br>*eel/lah...payr dooay jornee* |
| How much is that per day/week? | Quanto costa al giorno/alla settimana?<br>*Kwahnto kostah ahl jorno/ahllah saytteemahnah?* |
| How much is the deposit? | Quant'è la cauzione?<br>*Kwahnto ay lah kahootzeeonay?* |

| | |
|---|---|
| Could I have a receipt for the deposit? | Mi potrebbe dare una ricevuta per la cauzione?<br>*Mee potraybbay dahray oonah reechayhvootah payr lah kahootzeeonay?* |
| How much is the surcharge per kilometre? | Quant'è il supplemento di prezzo al chilometro?<br>*Kwahnto ay eel soopplaymaynto dee praytzo ahl keelomayhtro?* |
| Does that include petrol? | E' compresa la benzina?<br>*Ay kompraysah lah bayndzeenah?* |
| Does that include insurance? | E' compresa l'assicurazione?<br>*Ay compraysah laysseekoorahtzeeonay?* |
| What time can I pick the...up? | A che ora potrei venire a prendere il/la...?<br>*Ah kay orah potrayee vayneeray ah prayndayray eel/lah...?* |
| When does the...have to be back? | A che ora dovrò riportare il/la...?<br>*Ah kay orah dovro reeportahray eel/lah...?* |
| Where's the petrol tank? | Dov'è il serbatoio?<br>*Dovay eel sayrbahtoeeo?* |
| What sort of fuel does it take? | Quale carburante occorre?<br>*Kwahlay kahrboorahntay okkorray?* |

## 5.10 Hitchhiking

| | |
|---|---|
| Where are you heading? | Dove va?<br>*Dovay vah?* |
| Can you give me a lift? | Mi dà un passaggio?<br>*Mee dah oon pahssahdjo?* |
| Can my friend (m/f) come too? | Darebbe un passaggio anche al mio amico/alla mia amica?<br>*Dahraybbay oon pahssahdjo ahnkay ahl meeo ahmeeko/ahllah meeah ahmeekah?* |
| I'd like to go to... | Voglio andare a...<br>*Vollyo ahndahray ah...* |
| Is that on the way to...? | Si trova sulla strada per...?<br>*See trovah soollah strahda payr...?* |
| Could you drop me off...? | Mi potrebbe far scendere...?<br>*Mee potraybbay fahr shayndayray...?* |
| Could you drop me off here? | Mi potrebbe far scendere qui?<br>*Mee potraybbay fahr shayndayray kwee?* |
| – at the entrance to the motorway? | – all'entrata dell'autostrada?<br>*– ahll'ayntrahtah dayllowtostrahdah?* |
| – in the centre? | – al centro?<br>*– ahl chayntro?* |
| – at the next intersection? | – al prossimo incrocio?<br>*– ahl prosseemo eenkrocheeo?* |
| Could you stop here, please? | Si potrebbe fermare qui per favore?<br>*See potraybbay fayrmahray kwee payr fahvoray?* |
| I'd like to get out here | Vorrei scendere qui<br>*Vorrayee shayndayray kwee* |
| Thanks for the lift | Grazie per il passaggio<br>*Grahtzeeay payr eel pahssahdjo* |

# Public transport

# 6 Public transport

## 6.1 In general

● **Bus tickets** are purchased at tobacconists, newspaper stands and automatic vending machines at major bus stops, then validated in a machine as you enter the bus. Single tickets be bought in blocks of 4. Milan and Rome also have an underground train (*metropolitana*). Venice is served by a water-bus (*vaporetto*). Tickets are purchased from booths at most landing stations and validated before you get on the boat. A 24-hour ticket is good value for unlimited travel. Venice also has a gondola service (*traghetto*) crossing the Grand Canal, costing very little.

| | |
|---|---|
| Il treno per...delle ore...viaggia con un ritardo di (circa)...minuti | The [time] train to...has been delayed by (about)...minutes |
| E' in arrivo sul binario...il treno per... | The train to...is now arriving at platform... |
| E' in arrivo sul binario...il treno proveniente da... | The train from...is now arriving at platform... |
| E' in partenza dal binario...il treno per... | The train to...will leave from platform... |
| Oggi il treno per... delle ore...partirà dal binario... | Today the [time] train to...will leave from platform... |
| La prossima stazione è... | The next station is... |

| | |
|---|---|
| Where does this train go to? | Dove va questo treno?<br>*Dovay vah kwaysto trayno?* |
| Does this boat go to...? | Questo traghetto va a...?<br>*Kwaysto trahgaytto vah ah...?* |
| Can I take this bus to...? | Posso prendere questo autobus per andare a...?<br>*Posso prayndayray kwaysto ahootoboos payr ahndahray ah...?* |
| Does this train stop at...? | Questo treno si ferma a...?<br>*Kwaysto trayno see fayrmah ah...?* |
| Is this seat taken/free /reserved? | E' occupato/libero/prenotato questo posto?<br>*Ay okkoopahto/leebayro/praynotahto kwaysto posto?* |
| I've booked... | Ho prenotato...<br>*O praynotahto...* |
| Could you tell me where I have to get off for... ? | Mi potrebbe indicare la fermata per...?<br>*Mee potraybbay eendeekahray lah fayrmahtah payr...?* |
| Could you let me know when we get to...? | Mi potrebbe avvisare quando arriviamo a...?<br>*Mee potraybbay ahvveezahray kwahndo ahrreeveeahmo ah...?* |

| | |
|---|---|
| Could you stop at the next stop, please? | Si potrebbe fermare alla prossima fermata?<br>*See potraybbay fayrmahray ahllah prosseemah fayrmahtah?* |
| Where are we? | Dove siamo?<br>*Dovay seeahmo?* |
| Do I have to get off here? | Devo scendere adesso?<br>*Dayvo shayndayray ahdaysso?* |
| Have we already passed...? | Abbiamo già passato...?<br>*Ahbbeeahmo jah pahssahto ..?* |
| How long have I been asleep? | Quanto tempo ho dormito?<br>*Kwahnto taympo o dormeeto?* |
| How long does the train stop here? | Quanto tempo si fermerà il treno?<br>*Kwahnto taympo see fayrmayrah eel trayno?* |
| Can I come back on the same ticket? | Questo biglietto è valido anche per il viaggio di ritorno?<br>*Kwaysto beellyaytto ay vahleedo ahnkay payr eell veeahdjo dee reetorno?* |
| Can I change on this ticket? | Posso cambiare con questo biglietto?<br>*Posso kahmbeeahray con kwaysto beellyaytto?* |
| How long is this ticket valid for? | Quanto tempo è valido questo biglietto?<br>*Kwahnto taympo ay vahleedo kwaysto beellyaytto?* |
| How much is the supplement for the high speed train? | Quant'è il supplemento rapido?<br>*Kwahntò ay eel soopplaymaynto rahpeedo?* |

## 6.2 Questions to passengers

***Ticket types***

| | |
|---|---|
| Prima o seconda classe? | First or second class? |
| Andata o andata e ritorno? | Single or return? |
| Fumatori o non fumatori? | Smoking or non-smoking? |
| Vicino al finestrino? | Window seat? |
| In testa o in coda? | Front or back (of train)? |
| Un posto o una cuccetta? | Seat or couchette? |
| Sopra, in mezzo o sotto? | Top, middle or bottom? |
| Classe turistica o prima classe? | Economy or first class? |
| Una cabina o un posto a sedere? | Cabin or seat? |
| Una cabina singola o per due? | Single or double? |
| Quanti siete a viaggiare? | How many are travelling? |

***Destination***

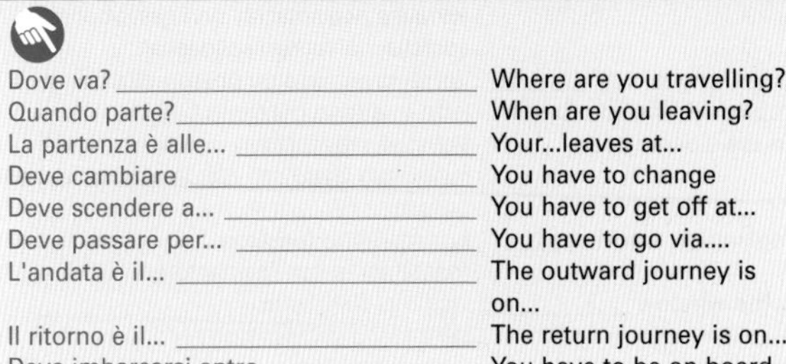

| | |
|---|---|
| Dove va? | Where are you travelling? |
| Quando parte? | When are you leaving? |
| La partenza è alle... | Your...leaves at... |
| Deve cambiare | You have to change |
| Deve scendere a... | You have to get off at... |
| Deve passare per... | You have to go via.... |
| L'andata è il... | The outward journey is on... |
| Il ritorno è il... | The return journey is on... |
| Deve imbarcarsi entro... | You have to be on board by....(o'clock) |

***Inside the vehicle***

| | |
|---|---|
| Biglietti prego | Tickets, please |
| La prenotazione prego | Your reservation, please |
| Passaporto prego | Your passport, please |
| Ha sbagliato posto | You're in the wrong seat |
| Ha sbagliato... | You have made a mistake/You are in the wrong... |
| Questo posto è prenotato | This seat is reserved |
| Deve pagare un supplemento | You'll have to pay a supplement |
| Il/la... viaggia con un ritardo di... minuti | The...has been delayed by...minutes |

## 6.3 Tickets

| | |
|---|---|
| Where can I...? | Dove posso...?<br>*Dovay posso...?* |
| – buy a ticket? | Dove posso comprare un biglietto?<br>*– komprahray oon beellyaytto?* |
| – reserve a seat? | Dove posso prenotare un posto?<br>*– praynotahray oon posto?* |
| – book a flight? | Dove posso prenotare un volo?<br>*– praynotahray oon volo?* |
| Could I have...for... please? | Mi può dare...per...per favore<br>*Mee pwo dahray...payr...payr fahvoray* |
| A single to...please | Un'andata per...per favore<br>*Oonahndahtah payr...payr fahvoray* |
| A return ticket, please | Un'andata e ritorno, per favore<br>*Oonahndahtah ay reetorno payr fahvoray* |
| first class | prima classe<br>*preemah klahssay* |
| second class | seconda classe<br>*saykondah klahssay* |
| economy class | classe turistica<br>*klahssay tooreesteekah* |

| | |
|---|---|
| I'd like to book a seat/couchette/cabin | Vorrei prenotare un posto/una cuccetta/una cabina<br>*Vorrayee praynotahray oon posto/oonah cootchayttah/oonah kahbeenah* |
| I'd like to book a top/middle/bottom berth in the sleeping car | Vorrei prenotare un posto nella carrozza letto in alto/in mezzo/in basso<br>*Vorrayee praynotahray oon posto nayllah kahrrotzah laytto een ahlto/een maydzo/een bahsso* |
| smoking/no smoking | fumatori/non fumatori<br>*foomahtoree/non foomahtoree* |
| by the window | vicino al finestrino<br>*veecheeno ahl feenaystreeno* |
| single/double | singola/per due<br>*seengolah/payr dooay* |
| at the front/back | nella parte davanti/in fondo<br>*nayllah pahrtay dahvahntee/een fondo* |
| There are...of us | Siamo in...<br>*Seeahmo een...* |
| We have a car | Abbiamo una macchina<br>*Ahbbeeahmo oonae makkeenah* |
| We have a caravan | Abbiamo una roulotte<br>*Ahbbeeahmo oonah roolot* |
| We have...bicycles | Abbiamo...biciclette<br>*Ahbbeeahmo...beecheeklayttay* |
| Do you have a... | Ha un/una ?<br>*Ah oon/oonah...?* |
| – travel card for 10 trips? | Ha una tessera valida dieci corse?<br>*Ah oonah tayssayrah vahleedah deeaychee corsay?* |
| – weekly travel card? | Ha un abbonamento settimanale<br>*Ah oon ahbbonahmaynto saytteemahnahlay?* |
| – monthly season ticket? | Ha un abbonamento mensile?<br>*Ah oon ahbbonahmaynto maynseelay?* |
| Where's-? | Dov'è ?<br>*Dovay ay?* |
| Where's the information desk? | Dov'è l'ufficio informazioni?<br>*Dovay ay looffeecheeo eenformahtzeeonee?* |

## 6.4 Information

| | |
|---|---|
| Where can I find a timetable? | Dov'è l'orario delle partenze/degli arrivi?<br>*Dovay ay lorayryo dayllay pahrtayntzay/daylly ahrreevee?* |
| Where's the...desk? | Dov'è il banco di...<br>*Dovay eel bahnko dee...* |
| Do you have a city map with the bus/the underground routes on it? | Avrebbe una pianta della città con le linee degli autobus/del metrò?<br>*Ahvraybbay oonah peeahntah dayllah cheettah kon lay leenayay daylly ahootoboos/dayl maytro?* |
| Do you have a timetable? | Avrebbe un orario?<br>*Ahvraybbay oon orayreeo?* |
| Will I get my money back? | Le spese mi saranno rimborsate?<br>*Lay spaysay mee sahrahnno reemborsahtay?* |

|  |  |
|---|---|
| I'd like to confirm/cancel/change my booking for/trip to... | Vorrei confermare/annullare/cambiare la prenotazione per...<br>*Vorrayee confayrmahray/ahnnoollahray/kahmbyahray lah praynotahtzeeonay payr...* |
| I'd like to go to... What is the quickest way to get there? | Vorrei andare a...Qual'è il modo più rapido per andarci?<br>*Vorrayee ahndahray ah...Kwahlay ay eel modo peeoo rahpeedo payr ahndahrchee?* |
| How much is a single/return to...? | Quanto costa un'andata/un'andata e ritorno per...?<br>*Kwahnto kostah oonahndahtah/oonahndahtah ay reetorno payr...?* |
| Do I have to pay a supplement? | Devo pagare un supplemento?<br>*Dayvo pahgahray oon soopplaymaynto?* |
| Can I break my journey with this ticket? | Posso interrompere il viaggio con questo biglietto?<br>*Posso eentayrrompayray eel veeahdjo con kwaysto beellyaytto?* |
| How much luggage am I allowed? | Quanti chili di bagaglio posso portare ?<br>*Kwahntee keely dee bahgahllyo posso portahray?* |
| Is this a direct train? | E' un treno diretto?<br>*Ay oon trayno deeraytto?* |
| Do I have to change? Where? | Devo cambiare? Dove?<br>*Dayvo kahmbeeahray? Dovay?* |
| Does the plane touch down anywhere? | L'aereo fa scalo da nessuna parte?<br>*Lahayrayo fah skahlo dah nayssoonah pahrtay?* |
| Will there be any stopovers? | Ci saranno soste intermedie?<br>*Chee sahrahnno sostay eentayrmaydeeay?* |
| Does the boat stop at any other ports on the way? | Il traghetto fa scalo ad altri porti?<br>*Eel trahgaytto fah skahlo ahdahltree portee?* |
| Does the train/bus stop at...? | Questo treno/autobus si ferma a...?<br>*Kwaysto trayno/ahootoboos see fayrmah ah...?* |
| Where do I get off? | Dove devo scendere?<br>*Dovay dayvo shayndayray?* |
| Is there a connection to...? | C'è una coincidenza per...?<br>*Chay oonah coeencheedayntzah payr...?* |
| How long do I have to wait? | Quanto tempo devo aspettare?<br>*Kwahnto taympo dayvo ahspayttahray?* |
| When does...leave? | Quando parte...?<br>*Kwahndo pahrtay...?* |
| What time does the first/next/last...leave? | A che ora parte il/la primo/a/il/la prossimo/a/l'ultimo/a...?<br>*Ah kay orah pahrtay eel/lah preemo/ah eel/lah prosseemo/ah/loolteemo/ah...?* |
| How long does...take? | Quanto tempo impiega...?<br>*Kwahnto taympo eempeeaygah...?* |
| What time does...arrive in...? | A che ora arriverà...a...?<br>*Ah kay orah ahrreevayhrah...ah...?* |
| Where does the...to... leave from? | Da dove parte il/la...per...?<br>*Dah dovay pahrtay eel/lah...payr...?* |
| Is this the train/bus...to...? | E' questo il treno/l'autobus per...?<br>*Ay kwaysto eel trayno/lahootoboos payr...?* |

## .5 Aeroplanes

● **On arrival** at an Italian airport (*aeroporto*), you will find the following signs:

| | | |
|---|---|---|
| accettazione<br>check-in | internazionale<br>international | voli domestici<br>domestic flights |
| arrivo<br>arrivals | partenze<br>departures | |

## .6 Trains

● **Train travel** in Italy is simple and cheap. *The Ferrovie dello Stato* (FS) is the state rail system. There are several types of trains: the *regionale* stops at all stations and is slow; the *interregionale* travels between regions; the *diretto* means you reach your destination without having to change; the *espresso* stops at major stations. The ETR450, or *Pendolino*, is an espress service between Rome, Florence, Bologna and Milan; the *Intercity* services major cities and the *EuroCity* connects major European cities. Tickets must be punched by a validation machine at the entrance to platforms.

## .7 Taxis

● **There are plenty of taxis** in Italian cities but they are quite expensive. They can be found on ranks, especially at train and bus stations, or you can phone the radio-taxi numbers from a rank or any telephone. Rates vary and there is a supplement from 10 pm to 7am and on Sundays and bank holidays. Check for airport supplements.

| | | |
|---|---|---|
| libero<br>for hire | occupato<br>occupied | posteggio dei taxi<br>taxi rank |

| | |
|---|---|
| Taxi! | Taxi!<br>*Tahxee!* |
| Could you get me a taxi, please? | Mi potrebbe chiamare un taxi?<br>*Mee potraybbay keeahmahray oon tahxee?* |
| Where can I find a taxi around here? | Dove posso prendere un taxi qui vicino?<br>*Dovay posso prayndayray oon tahxee kwee veecheeno?* |
| Could you take me to..., please? | Mi porti a... per favore<br>*Mee portee ah...payr fahvoray* |
| Could you take me to this address, please | Mi porti a questo indirizzo per favore<br>*Mee portee ah kwaysto eendeereetzo payr fahvoray* |
| – to the...hotel, please | Mi porti all'albergo...per favore<br>*Mee portee ahllahlbayrgo...payr fahvoray* |
| – to the town/city centre, please | Mi porti al centro per favore<br>*Mee portee ahl chayntro payr fahvoray* |
| – to the station, please | Mi porti alla stazione per favore<br>*Mee portee ahllah statzeeonay payr fahvoray* |

| | |
|---|---|
| – to the airport, please | Mi porti all'aeroporto per favore<br>*Mee portee ahllahayroporto payr fahvoray* |
| How much is the trip to...? | Quanto costa una corsa fino a...?<br>*Kwahnto kostah oonah korsah feeno ah...?* |
| How far is it to...? | Quanto è lontano...?<br>*Kwahnto ay lontahno...?* |
| Could you turn on the meter, please? | Può accendere il tassametro, per piacere?<br>*Pwo ahtchayndayray eel tahssahmaytro, payr peeahchayray?* |
| I'm in a hurry | Ho fretta<br>*O frayttah* |
| Could you speed up/ slow down a little? | Può andare più veloce/piano?<br>*Pwo ahndahray peeoo vayhlochay/peeahno?* |
| Could you take a different route? | Può prendere un'altra strada?<br>*Pwo prayndayray oonahltrah strahdah?* |
| I'd like to get out here, please. | Mi faccia scendere adesso<br>*Mee fahtchhah shayndayray ahdaysso* |
| Go - | Vada<br>*Vahdah* |
| You have to go...here | Deve andare... qui<br>*Dayvay ahndahray... kwee* |
| Go straight ahead | Vada dritto<br>*Vahdah dreetto* |
| Turn left | Vada a sinistra<br>*Vahda ah seeneestra* |
| Turn right | Vada a destra<br>*Vahdah ah daystrah* |
| This is it/We're here | Siamo arrivati<br>*Seeahmo ahrreevahtee* |
| Could you wait a minute for me, please? | Mi potrebbe aspettare un attimo?<br>*Mee potraybbay ahspayttahray oon ahtteemo?* |

# Overnight accommodation

# Overnight accommodation

## 7.1 General

● **There is a great variety** of overnight accommodation in Italy and prices vary according to the season.

A hotel or *albergo* can be awarded up to five stars while a *pensione* will usually be one-three star quality. *Locande* are similar to *pensioni*, and *alloggi* or *affittacamere* are usually cheaper and are not part of the star classification system. Youth hostels, *ostelli per la gioventù*, are often in beautiful locations. Some hostels offer family rooms. *Agriturismo* is the increasingly popular practice of staying in farmhouses, at a restaurant with rooms to rent or perhaps in a restored medieval farm complex. Some religious institutions, *casa religiosa di ospitalità*, offer accommodation equivalent to a one-star hotel. There is a network of *rifugi* offering dormitory accommodation in the Alps, Appenines or other mountains in Italy. Campsites range from large complexes with swimming pools, tennis courts, restaurants etc. to simple grounds. Free camping is generally not permitted in Italy and you need the permission of the landowner if you want to camp on private property.

| | |
|---|---|
| Quanto tempo vuole rimanere? | How long will you be staying? |
| Mi compili questo modulo, per favore | Fill out this form, please |
| Potrei avere il Suo passaporto? | Could I see your passport? |
| Deve pagare una caparra | I'll need a deposit |
| Deve pagare in anticipo | You'll have to pay in advance |

| | |
|---|---|
| My name is...I've made a reservation | Il mio nome è...Ho prenotato<br>*Eel meeo nomay ay...O praynotahto* |
| How much is it per night/week/ month? | Quanto costa per una notte/alla settimana/al mese?<br>*Kwahnto kostah payr oonah nottay/ahllah saytteemahnah/ahl maysay?* |
| We'll be staying at least...nights/weeks | Vogliamo rimanere minimo...notti/settimane<br>*Vollyahmo reemahnayray meeneemo...nottee/setteemahnay* |
| We don't know yet | Non lo sappiamo di preciso<br>*Non lo sahppeeahmo dee praycheezo* |
| Do you allow pets (cats/dogs)? | Sono permessi gli animali domestici (cani/gatti)?<br>*Sono payrmayssee lly ahneemahlee domaysteechee (kahnee/gahttee)?* |
| What time does the gate/door open/close? | A che ora apre/chiude il cancello?<br>*Ah kay orah ahpray/keeooday eel kahnchello?* |
| Could you get me a taxi, please? | Mi potrebbe chiamare un taxi?<br>*Mee potraybbay keeahmahray oon tahxee?* |
| Is there any mail for me? | C'è posta per me?<br>*Chay postah payr may?* |

## Camping equipment

(the diagram shows the numbered parts)

| | | | |
|---|---|---|---|
| | luggage space | lo spazio per bagaglio | *lo spahzeeo payr bahgahllyo* |
| | can opener | apriscatole (m) | *ahpreeskahtolay* |
| | butane gas bottle | bombola a gas butano | *bombolah ah gahs bootahno* |
| 1 | pannier | sacca | *sahkkah* |
| 2 | gas cooker | fornello da campeggio | *fornayllo dah kahmpaydjeeo* |
| 3 | groundsheet | fondo della tenda | *fondo dayllah tayndah* |
| | mallet | martello di gomma | *mahrtayllo dee gommah* |
| | hammock | amaca | *ahmahkah* |
| 4 | jerry can | tanica | *tahneekah* |
| | campfire | fuoco | *fwoko* |
| 5 | folding chair | seggiolino pieghevole | *saydjoleeno peeaygayvolay* |
| 6 | insulated picnic box | borsa frigo | *borsah freego* |
| | ice pack | accumulatore (m) di ghiaccio | *ahkkoomoolahtoray dee geeahtcheeo* |
| | compass | bussola | *boossolah* |
| | corkscrew | cavatappi | *kahvahtahppee* |
| 7 | airbed | materassino gonfiabile | *mahtayrahsseeno gonfeeahbeelay* |
| 8 | airbed pump | pompa | *pompah* |
| 9 | awning | tenda | *tayndah* |
| 10 | sleeping bag | sacco a pelo | *sahkko ah paylo* |
| 11 | saucepan | pentola | *payntohlah* |
| 12 | handle (pan) | manico | *mahneeko* |
| | primus stove | fornello a spirito | *fornayllo ah speereeto* |
| | zip | chiusura lampo | *keeoozoorah lahmpo* |
| 13 | backpack | zaino | *dzaheeno* |
| 14 | guy rope | tirante (m) di tenda | *teerahntay dee tayndah* |
| 15 | storm lantern | lanterna a vento | *lahntayrnah ah vaynto* |
| | camp bed | brandina | *brahndeenah* |
| | table | tavolino | *tahvoleeno* |
| 16 | tent | tenda | *tayndah* |
| 17 | tent peg | picchetto | *peekkaytto* |
| 18 | tent pole | palo | *pahloh* |
| | thermos flask | il termos | *eel tayrmoss* |
| 19 | water bottle | borraccia | *borrahtchah* |
| | clothes peg | molletta | *mollayttah* |
| | clothes line | corda da bucato | *kordah dah bookahto* |
| | windbreak | paravento | *pahrahvaynto* |
| 20 | torch | torcia | *torchah* |
| | penknife | temperino | *taympayreeno* |

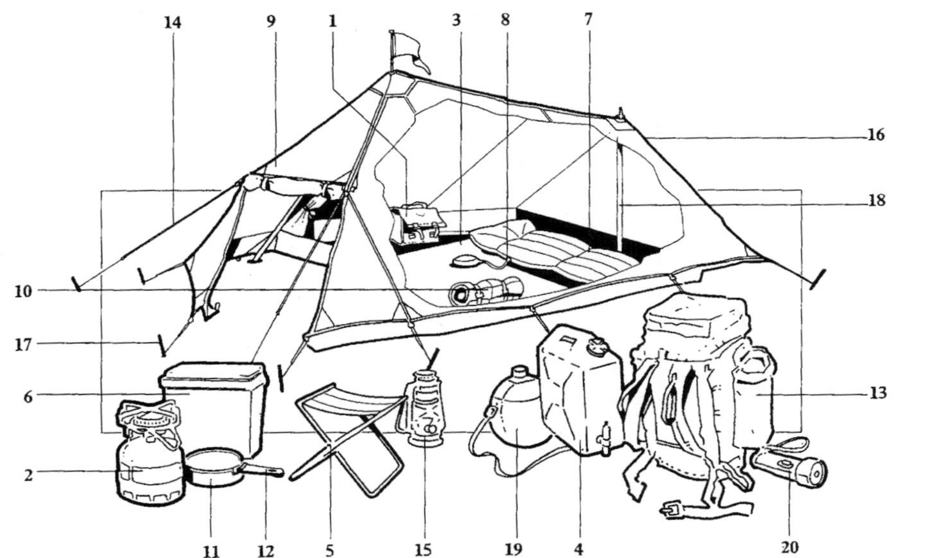
14
9
1
3
8
7
16
18
10
17
6
13
2
11
12
5
15
19
4
20

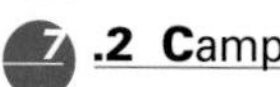

## 7.2 Camping

*See the diagram on page 69.*

| | |
|---|---|
| Scelga pure un posto | You can pick your own site |
| Le verrà indicato un posto | You'll be allocated a site |
| Ecco il numero del Suo posto | This is your site number. |
| Attacchi bene questo sulla macchina per favore | Please stick this firmly to your car |
| Non perda questa tesserina | You mustn't lose this card |

| | |
|---|---|
| Where's the manager? | Dov'è l'amministratore?<br>*Dovay ay lahmmeenneestrahtoray?* |
| Are we allowed to camp here? | E' permesso fare il campeggio qui?<br>*Ay payrmaysso fahray eel kahmpaydjo kwee?* |
| There are...of us and we have...tents | Siamo in...e abbiamo...tende<br>*Seeahmo een...ay ahbbeeahmo...taynday* |
| Can we pick our own site? | Possiamo scegliere noi un posto?<br>*Posseeahmo shayllyayhray noee oon posto?* |
| Do you have a quiet spot for us? | Ha un posto tranquillo per noi?<br>*Ah oon posto trahnkweello payr noy?* |
| Do you have any other sites available? | Non c'è un altro posto libero?<br>*Non chay oonahltro posto leebayro?* |
| It's too windy/sunny/ shady here. | C'è troppo vento/troppo sole/troppa ombra qui<br>*Chay troppo vaynto/troppo solay/troppah ombrah kwee* |
| It's too crowded here | C'è troppa gente qui<br>*Chay troppah jayntay kwee* |
| The ground's too hard/uneven | La terra è troppo dura/ineguale<br>*Lah tayhrrah ay troppo doorah/eenaygwahlay* |
| Do you have a level spot for the camper/caravan/folding caravan? | Ha un posto piano per il nostro camper/la nostra roulotte/il nostro carrello tenda?<br>*Ah oon posto peeahno payr eel nostro kahmper/lah nostrah roolot/eel nostro kahrrayllo tayndah?* |
| Could we have adjoining sites? | E' possibile avere posti vicini?<br>*Ay posseebeelay ahvayray postee veecheenee?* |
| Can we park the car next to the tent? | E' permesso parcheggiare la macchina vicino alla tenda?<br>*Ay payrmaysso pahrkaydjahray lah mahkkeenah veecheeno ahllah tayndah?* |
| How much is it per person/tent/caravan/car? | Quanto costa per persona/per una tenda/per una roulotte/per una macchina?<br>*Kwahnto kostah payr payrsonah/payr oonah tayndah/payr oonah roolot/payr oonah mahkkeenah?* |
| Do you have chalets for hire? | Ha uno chalet da affittare?<br>*Ah oono shahlay dah ahffeettahray?* |
| Are there any...? | Ci sono...?<br>*Chee sono...?* |

– hot showers?
Ci sono docce calde?
*Chee sono dotchay kahlday?*

– washing machines?
Ci sono lavatrici?
*Chee sono lahvahtreechee?*

Is there a...on the site?
Il campeggio ha...?
*Eel kahmpaydjo ah...?*

Is there a children's play area on the site?
Il campeggio ha un parco giochi?
*Eel kamppaydjo ah oon pahrko jokee?*

Are there covered cooking facilities on the site?
C'è un' area coperta per cucinare?
*Chay oonahrayah kopayrtah payr koocheenahray?*

Can I rent a safe?
E' possibile prendere a noleggio una cassetta di sicurezza?
*Ay posseebeelay prayndayray ah nolaydjo oonah kahssayttah dee seekooraytzah?*

Are we allowed to barbecue here?
E' permesso fare il barbecue?
*Ay payrmaysso fahray eel bahrbaykeeoo?*

Are there any power points?
Ci sono delle prese elettriche?
*Chee sono dayllay praysay aylayttreekay?*

Is there drinking water?
C'è acqua potabile?
*Chay ahkwah potahbeelay?*

When's the rubbish collected?
Quando c'è la raccolta dei rifiuti?
*Kwahndo chay lah rahkkoltah dayèe reefeeootee?*

Do you sell gas bottles (butane gas/propane gas)?
Vende delle bombole di gas (gas butano/gas propano)?
*Vaynday dayllay bombolay dee gahs (gahs bootahno/gahs propahno)?*

## 7.3 Hotel/B&B/apartment/holiday house

Do you have a single/double room available?
Ha una camera singola/doppia?
*Ah oonah kahmayhrah seengolah/doppeeah?*

per person/per room
per persona/per camera
*payr payrsonah/payr kahmayhrah*

Does that include breakfast/lunch/dinner?
E' inclusa la prima colazione?/E' incluso il pranzo?/E' inclusa la cena?
*Ay eenkloosah lah preemah kolahtzeeonay?/Ay eenklooso eel prahntzo?/Ay eenkloosah lah chaynah?*

Could we have two adjoining rooms?
E' possibile stare in due camere vicine?
*Ay posseebeelay stahray een dooay kahmayray veecheenay?*

with/without toilet/bath/shower
con/senza gabinetto/bagno/doccia
*con/saynzah gahbeenaytto/bahneeo/dotchah*

facing the street
guarda sulla strada
*gwahrdah soollah strahdah*

at the back
sul retro
*sool raytro*

with/without sea view
che dà/che non dà sul mare
*kay dah/kay non dah sool mahray*

Is there...in the hotel?
L'albergo ha...?
*Lahlbayrgo hah...?*

Is there a lift in the hotel?
L'albergo ha l'ascensore?
*Lahlbayrgo ah lahshaynsoray?*

Do you have room service?
C'è il servizio in camera?
*Chay eel sayrveetzeeo een kahmayhrah?*

| | |
|---|---|
| Could I see the room? | E' possibile vedere la camera? *Ay posseebeelay vahdayray lah kahmayrah?* |
| I'll take this room | Prendo questa *Prayndo kwaystah* |

| | |
|---|---|
| Il bagno e la doccia sono allo stesso piano/nella Sua càmera | The toilet and shower are on the same floor/en suite |
| Prego, da questa parte | This way please |
| La Sua camera è al...piano, numero... | Your room is on the...floor, number... |

| | |
|---|---|
| We don't like this one | Questa qui non ci piace *Kwaystah kwee non chee peeahchay* |
| Do you have a larger/less expensive room? | Ha una camera più grande/meno cara? *Ah oonah kahmayhrah peeoo grahnday/mayno kahrah?* |
| Could you put in a cot? | Potrebbe aggiungere un lettino per il bambino/la bambina? *Potraybbay ahdjoonjayray oon laytteeno payr eel bahmbeeno/lah bahmbeenah?* |
| What time's breakfast? | A che ora c'è la colazione? *Ah kay orah chay lah kolahtzeeonay?* |
| Where's the dining room? | Dov'è la sala da pranzo? *Dovay ay la sahlah dah prahntzo?* |
| Can I have breakfast in my room? | Mi potrebbe portare la prima colazione in camera? *Mee potraybbay portahray lah preemah kolahtzeeonay een kahmayhrah?* |
| Where's the emergency exit/fire escape? | Dov'è l'uscita di sicurezza/la scala di sicurezza? *Dovay ay loosheetah dee seekooraytzah/lah skahlah dee seekooretzah?* |
| Where can I park my car (safely)? | Dove posso parcheggiare la mia macchina (in un posto sicuro)? *Dovay posso pahrkaydjahray lah meeah mahkkeenah (een oon posto seekooro)?* |
| The key to room..., please | La chiave della camera...per favore *Lah keeahvay dayllah kahmayhrah...payr fahvoray* |
| Could you put this in the safe, please? | Posso mettere questo nella sua cassetta di sicurezza? *Posso mayttayray kwaysto naylla sooah kahssayttah dee seekooraytzah?* |
| Could you wake me at...tomorrow? | Mi potrebbe svegliare domani alle...? *Mee potraybbay svayllyahray domahnee ahllay...?* |
| Could you find a babysitter for me? | Mi potrebbe cercare una babysitter? *Mee potraybbay chayrkahray oonah bahbeeseettayr?* |
| Could I have an extra blanket? | Potrei avere un'altra coperta? *Potray ahvayhray oonahltrah copayrtah?* |
| What days do the cleaners come in? | Che giorno fanno le pulizie? *Kay jorno fahnno lay pooleetzeeay?* |

|  |  |  |
|---|---|---|
| When are the sheets/ towels/tea towels changed? | Quando cambiano le lenzuola/gli asciugamani/gli strofinacci? | *Kwahndo kahmbeeahno lay layntzwolah/lly ahshoogahmahnee/lly strofeenahtchee?* |

## .4 Complaints

|  |  |  |
|---|---|---|
| We can't sleep for the noise | Non riusciamo a dormire per i rumori | *Non reeoosheeahmo ah dormeeray payr ee roomoree* |
| Could you turn the radio down, please? | Può abbassare la radio? | *Pwo ahbbahssahray lah rahdeeo?* |
| We're out of toilet paper | E' finita la carta igienica | *Ay feeneetah lah kahrtah eejayneekah* |
| There aren't any.../ there's not enough... | Non ci sono/ci sono troppo pochi/e... | *Non chee sono/chee sono troppo pokee/ay...* |
| The bed linen's dirty | La biancheria è sporca | *Lah beeahnkayreeyah ay sporkah* |
| The room hasn't been cleaned. | La camera non è stata pulita | *La kahmayrah non ay stahtah pooleetah* |
| The kitchen is not clean | La cucina non è pulita | *Lah koocheenah non ay pooleetah* |
| The kitchen utensils are dirty | Gli utensili da cucina sono sporchi | *Lly ootaynseelee dah koocheenah sono sporkee* |
| The heating isn't working | Il riscaldamento non funziona | *Eel reeskahldahmaynto non foontzeeonah* |
| There's no (hot) water/electricity | Non c'è acqua (calda)/corrente | *Non chay ahkwah (kahldah)/corrayntay* |
| ...doesn't work/is broken | ...non funziona/è rotto/a | *...non foontzeeonah/ay rotto/ah* |
| Could you have that seen to? | Potrebbe farlo aggiustare? | *Potraybbay fahrlo ahdjoostahray?* |
| Could I have another room/site? | Posso cambiare camera/posto per la tenda? | *Posso kahmbeeahray kahmayra/posto payr lah tayndah?* |
| The bed creaks terribly | Il letto scricchiola terribilmente | *Eel laytto skreekkeeolah tayrreebeelmayntay* |
| The bed sags | Il letto cede troppo | *Eel laytto chayday troppo* |
| Could I have a board under the mattress? | Mi potrebbe dare una tavola da mettere sotto il materasso? | *Mee potraybbay dahray oonah tahvolah dah mayttayray sotto eel mahtayrahsso?* |
| It's too noisy | C'è troppo rumore | *Chay troppo roomoray* |
| There are a lot of insects/bugs | Ci sono molti insetti | *Chee sono moltee eensayttee* |
| This place is full of mosquitos | E' pieno di zanzare | *Ay peeayno dee zahnzahray* |
| – cockroaches | E' pieno di scarafaggi | *Ay peeayno dee skahrahfahdjee* |

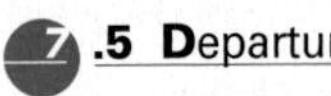

## 7.5 Departure

**See also 8.2 Settling the bill**

I'm leaving tomorrow. Could I settle my bill, please? — Domani parto. Mi potrebbe fare il conto adesso?
*Domahny pahrto. Mee potraybbay fahray eel konto ahdaysso?*

What time should we vacate the room? — A che ora dobbiamo lasciare la camera?
*Ah kay orah dobbeeahmo lahsheeahray lah kahmayhrah?*

Could I have my deposit/passport back, please? — Mi potrebbe riconsegnare la caparra/il passaporto?
*Mee potraybbay reekonsayneeahray lah kahpahrrah/eel pahssahporto?*

We're in a great hurry — Abbiamo molta fretta
*Abbeeahrmo moltah frayttah*

Could you forward my mail to this address? — Può rispedirmi la posta a questo indirizzo?
*Pwo reespaydeermee lah postah ah kwaysto eendeereetzo?*

Could we leave our luggage here until we leave? — Possiamo lasciare le nostre valigie qui finchè partiamo?
*Posseeahmo lahsheeahray lay nostray vahleedjay kwee feenkay pahrteeahmo?*

Thanks for your hospitality — Grazie per l'ospitalità
*Grahtzeeay payr lospeetahleetah*

# Money matters

# Money matters

● **In general,** banks are open to the public Monday to Friday from 8:30am to 1:30pm, and 2:30 to 4:30pm, but it is always possible to find an exchange office *(cambio)* open in larger towns or tourist centres. Proof of identity is usually required to exchange currency.

## 8.1 Banks

| | |
|---|---|
| Where can I find a bank/an exchange office around here? | Scusi, c'è una banca/un'agenzia di cambio qui vicino? *Skoozee, chay oonah bahnkah/ oonahjayntzeeah dee kahmbeeo kwee veecheeno?* |
| Where can I cash this traveller's cheque/giro cheque? | Dove posso incassare questo traveller cheque/assegno postale? *Dovay posso eenkahssahray kwaysto trahvayllayr shayk/ahssayneeo postahlay?* |
| Can I cash this...here? | E' possibile incassare qui questo/a... *Ay posseebeelay eenkahssahray kwee kwaysto/ah...?* |
| Can I withdraw money on my credit card here? | E' possibile prelevare qui dei soldi con una carta di credito? *Ay posseebeelay praylayvahray kwee dayee soldee con oonah kahrtah dee craydeeto?* |
| What's the minimum/ maximum amount? | Qual'è la somma minima/massima? *Kwahlay ay lah sommah meeneemah/ mahsseemah?* |
| Can I take out less than that? | E' possibile prelevare una somma minore? *Ay posseebeelay praylayvahray oonah sommah meenoray?* |
| I had some money cabled here. Has it arrived yet? | Ho fatto fare una rimessa per cablogramma. E' già arrivata? *Oh fahtto fahray oona reemayssah payr kahblograhmmah. Ay jah ahrreevahtah?* |
| These are the details of my bank in the UK | Ecco i dati della mia banca in Inghilterra *Ekko ee dahtee dayllah meeah bahnkah een Eengeeltayhrrah* |
| This is the number of my bank/giro account | Ecco il numero del mio conto in banca/conto corrente postale *Ekko eel noomayro dayl meeo konto een bahnkah/konto korrayntay postahlay* |
| I'd like to change some money | Vorrei cambiare dei soldi *Vorrayee kahmbeeahray dayee soldee* |
| – pounds into... | – sterline in... *– stayrleenay een...* |
| – dollars into... | – dollari in... *– dollahree een...* |
| What's the exchange rate? | Quant'è il cambio? *Kwahnto ay eel kahmbeeo?* |
| Could you give me some small change with it? | Mi potrebbe dare anche degli spiccioli per favore? *Mee potraybbay dahray ahnkay daylly speetchohlee payr fahvoray?* |
| This is not right | C'è un errore *Chay oonayrroray* |

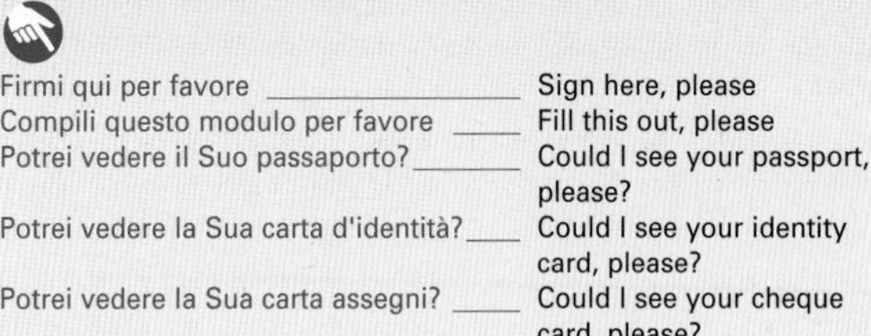

| | |
|---|---|
| Firmi qui per favore | Sign here, please |
| Compili questo modulo per favore | Fill this out, please |
| Potrei vedere il Suo passaporto? | Could I see your passport, please? |
| Potrei vedere la Sua carta d'identità? | Could I see your identity card, please? |
| Potrei vedere la Sua carta assegni? | Could I see your cheque card, please? |
| Potrei vedere la Sua carta assegni? | Could I see your bank card, please? |

## 8.2 Settling the bill

| | |
|---|---|
| Could you put it on my bill? | Lo metta sul mio conto<br>*Lo mayttah sool meeo konto* |
| Is service included? | Il servizio è compreso?<br>*Eel sayrveetzeeo ay komprayso?* |
| Can I pay by...? | Potrei pagare con...?<br>*Potrayee pahgahray kon...?* |
| Can I pay by credit card? | Potrei pagare con una carta di credito?<br>*Potrayee pahgahray kon oonah kahrtah dee kraydeeto?* |
| Can I pay by traveller's cheque? | Potrei pagare con un traveller cheque?<br>*Potrayee pahgahray kon oon trahvayller shayk?* |
| Can I pay with foreign currency? | Potrei pagare con soldi stranieri?<br>*Potrayee pahgahray kon soldee straneeayree?* |
| You've given me too much/you haven't given me enough change. | Mi ha dato troppo di resto/Non mi ha dato abbastanza di resto<br>*Mee ah dahto troppo dee raysto/Non mee ah dahto ahbbahstahnzah dee raysto* |
| Could you check this again, please? | Potrebbe verificare di nuovo?<br>*Potraybbay vayhreefeekahray dee nwovo?* |
| Could I have a receipt, please? | Mi potrebbe dare una ricevuta per favore?<br>*Mee potraybbay dahray oonah reechayvootah payr fahvoray?* |
| I don't have enough money on me. | Non mi bastano i soldi<br>*Non mee bahstahno ee soldee* |

| | |
|---|---|
| Non accettiamo carte di credito/traveller cheque/ valuta straniera | We don't accept credit cards/traveller's cheques/foreign currency |

| | |
|---|---|
| This is for you | Ecco a Lei<br>*Aykkoh ah lay* |
| Keep the change | Tenga il resto<br>*Tayngah eel raysto* |

# Post and telephone

# Post and telephone

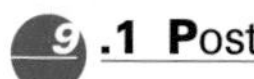

## 9.1 Post

***For giros, see 8 Money matters***

● **Major post offices** are open Monday to Saturday from 8:30am to 6 or 7pm. Smaller post offices open Monday to Friday, 8:30am to 2pm and on Saturdays from 8:30am to midday. Stamps *(francobolli)* can also be purchased at authorised tobacconists *(tabacchi).* The cost of sending a letter depends on its weight and the cost of sending an air mail letter also depends on where it is being sent. The Italian postal service is notoriously inefficient.

| | | |
|---|---|---|
| francobolli<br>stamps | telegrammi<br>telegrammes | vaglia postali<br>money orders |
| pacchi<br>parcels | | |

| | |
|---|---|
| Where is...? | Dov'è...?<br>*Dovay ay...?* |
| – the nearest post office? | Dov'è l'ufficio postale più vicino?<br>*Dovay ay looffeetcheeo postahlay peeoo veecheeno?* |
| – the main post office | Dov'è la posta centrale?<br>*Dovay ay lah postah chayntrahlay?* |
| – the nearest post box? | Dov'è la buca delle lettere più vicina?<br>*Dovay ay lah bookah dayllay layttayray peeoo veecheenah?* |
| Which counter should I go to...? | A quale sportello devo rivolgermi?<br>*Ah kwahlay sportayllo dayvo reevoljayrmee?* |
| Which counter should I go to to send a fax? | Lo sportello per fare un fax, qual è?<br>*Lo sportayllo payr fahray oon fahx, kwahlay?* |
| Which counter should I go to to change money? | Lo sportello per cambiare dei soldi, qual è?<br>*Lo sportayllo payr kahmbyahray dayee soldee, kwahlay?* |
| Which counter should I go to to change giro cheques? | Lo sportello per i vaglia di conto corrente postale, qual è?<br>*Lo sportayllo payr ee vahllyah dee konto korrayntay postahlay, kwahlay?* |
| Which counter should I go to to cable a money order? | Lo sportello per fare una rimessa cablografica, qual è?<br>*Lo sportayllo payr fahray oonah reemayssah kahblograhfeekah, kwahlay?* |
| Which counter should I go to for poste restante? | Lo sportello per il fermo posta, qual è?<br>*Lo sportayllo payr eel fayrmo postah, kwahlay?* |
| Is there any mail for me? My name's... | C'è posta per me? Il mio nome è...?<br>*Chay postah payr may? Eel meeo nomay ay...* |

***Stamps***

| | |
|---|---|
| What's the postage for a...to...? | Quanti francobolli ci vogliono per un/uno...da spedire a/in...? *Kwahntee frahnkobollee chee vollyono payr oon/oonah...dah spaydeeray ah/een...?* |
| Are there enough stamps on it? | Bastano questi francobolli? *Bahstahno kwaystee frahnkobollee?* |
| I'd like [quantity] [value] stamps | Vorrei...francobolli da... *Vorrayee...frahnkobollee dah...* |
| I'd like to send this... | Vorrei spedire questo/a... *Vorrayee spaydeeray kwaysto/ah...* |
| – express | Vorrei spedire questo/a per espresso *Vorrayee spaydeeray kwaysto/ah payr ayspraysso* |
| – by air mail | Vorrei spedire questo/a per posta aerea *Vorrayee spaydeeray kwaysto/ah payr postah ahayrayah* |
| – by registered mail | Vorrei spedire questo/a per raccomandata *Vorrayee spaydeeray kwaysto/ah payr rahkkomahndahtah* |

***Telegram / fax***

| | |
|---|---|
| I'd like to send a telegram to... | Vorrei spedire un telegramma a... *Vorrayee spaydeeray oon taylaygrahmmah ah...* |
| How much is that per word? | Quanto costa per parola? *Kwahnto kostah payr pahrolah?* |
| This is the text I want to send | Ecco il testo che vorrei spedire *Ekko eel taysto kay vorray spaydeeray* |
| Shall I fill out the form myself? | Desidera che compili io il modulo? *Dayzeedayhrah kay kompeelee eeo eel modoolo?* |
| Can I make photocopies/ send a fax here? | E' possibile fare una fotocopia qui/spedire un fax da qui? *Ay posseebeelay fahray oonah fotokopeeah kwee/spaydeeray oon fahx dah kwee?* |
| How much is it per page? | Quanto costa per pagina? *Kwahnto kostah payr pahjeenah?* |

## 9.2 Telephone

***See also 1.8 Telephone alphabet***

● **Direct international calls** can easily be made from public telephones using a phonecard available from tobacconists *(tabacchi)*, newspaper stands and vending machines in Telecom offices. Phonecards have a value of L 5,000, L 10,000 or L 15,000. Dial 00 to get out of Italy, then the relevant country code (UK 44; USA 1), city code and number. To make a reverse charge call from a public telephone, dial 170 for international and 15 for European countries. All operators speak English. When phoning someone in Italy, you will be greeted with *Pronto.*

| | |
|---|---|
| Is there a phone box around here? | Senta, c'è una cabina telefonica qui vicino?<br>*Sayntah, chay oonah kahbeenah taylayfoneekah kwee veecheeno?* |
| May I use your phone, please? | Scusi, potrei servirmi del Suo telefono?<br>*Skoozee, potrayee sayrveermee dayl soo-o taylayfono?* |
| Do you have a (city/region) phone directory? | Ha un elenco telefonico della città di/della regione...?<br>*Ah oonaylaynko taylayfoneeko dayllah cheettah dee..../dayllah rayjonay...?* |
| Where can I get a phone card? | Dove posso comprare una scheda telefonica?<br>*Dovay posso komprahray oonah skaydah taylayfoneekah?* |
| Could you give me...? | Mi potrebbe dare...?<br>*Mee potraybbay dahray...?* |
| – the number for international directory enquiries? | Mi potrebbe dare il numero dell'ufficio informazioni per l'estero?<br>*Mee potraybbay dahray eel noomayro dayll ooffeecheeo eenformahtzeeonee payr laystayro?* |
| – the number of room...? | Mi potrebbe dare il numero della camera...?<br>*Mee potraybbay dahray eel noomayro dayllah kahmayrah...?* |
| – the international access code? | Mi potrebbe dare il prefisso internazionale?<br>*Mee potraybbay dahray eel prayfeesso eentayrnahtzeeonahlay?* |
| – the...(country) code? | Mi potrebbe dare il prefisso per il/la...?<br>*Mee potraybbay dahray eel prayfeesso payr eel/lah...?* |
| – the trunk code for...? | Mi potrebbe dare il prefisso di...?<br>*Mee potraybbay dahray eel prayfeesso dee...?* |
| – the number of [subscriber]...? | Mi potrebbe dare il numero dell' abbonato...?<br>*Mee potraybbay dahray eel noomayro dayll ahbbonahto...?* |
| Could you check if this number's correct? | Potrebbe verificare se questo numero è giusto?<br>*Potraybbay vayhreefeekahray say kwaysto noomayro ay joosto?* |
| Can I dial international direct? | E' possibile chiamare direttamente all'estero?<br>*Ay posseebeelay keeahmahray deerayttahmayntay ahllaystayro?* |
| Do I have to go through the switchboard? | Bisogna chiamare tramite il centralino?<br>*Beezoneeah keeahmahray trahmeetay eel chayntrahleeno?* |
| Do I have to dial '0' first? | Bisogna prima fare lo zero?<br>*Beezoneeah preemah fahray lo dzayro?* |
| Do I have to book my calls? | Bisogna prenotare la telefonata?<br>*Beezoneeah praynotahray lah taylayfonahtah?* |

| | |
|---|---|
| Could you dial this number for me, please? | Mi potrebbe fare il seguente numero per favore?<br>*Mee potraybbay fahray eel saygwayntay noomayro payr fahvoray?* |
| Could you put me through to.../extension..., please? | Mi potrebbe passare.../interno numero...per favore?<br>*Mee potraybbay pahssahray.../eentayrno noomayro...payr fahvoray?* |
| I'd like to place a reverse charge call to... | Vorrei fare una telefonata a carico del destinatario, numero...<br>*Vorrayee fahray oonah taylayfonahtah ah kahreeko dayl daysteenahtahreeo, noomayro...* |
| What's the charge per minute? | Quanto costa al minuto?<br>*Kwahnto kostah ahl meenooto?* |
| Have there been any calls for me? | C'è stata una chiamata per me?<br>*Chay stahtah oonah keeahmahtah payr may?* |

***The conversation***

| | |
|---|---|
| Hello, this is... | Pronto, sono...<br>*Pronto, sono...* |
| Who is this, please? | Chi parla?<br>*Kee pahrlah?* |
| Is this...? | Parlo con...?<br>*Pahrlo kon...?* |
| I'm sorry, I've dialled the wrong number | Scusi, ho sbagliato numero<br>*Skoozee, o zbahllyahto noomayro* |
| I can't hear you | Non La sento<br>*Non lah saynto* |
| I'd like to speak to... | Vorrei parlare con...<br>*Vorrayee pahrlahray kon...* |
| Is there anybody who speaks English? | C'è qualcuno che parla inglese?<br>*Chay kwahlkoono kay pahrlah eenglaysay?* |
| Extension..., please | Mi passi l'interno numero...<br>*Mee pahssee leentayrno noomayro...* |

| | |
|---|---|
| La vogliono al telefono | There's a phone call for you |
| Bisogna prima fare lo zero | You have to dial '0' first |
| Un attimo per favore | One moment, please |
| Non risponde nessuno | There's no answer |
| Il numero è occupato | The line's engaged |
| Vuole aspettare? | Do you want to hold? |
| Le passo... | Putting you through |
| Ha sbagliato numero | You've got a wrong number |
| In questo momento non c'è | He's/she's not here right now |
| Tornerà alle... | He'll/she'll be back at... |
| Questa è la segreteria telefonica di... | This is the answering machine of... |

| | |
|---|---|
| Could you ask him/her to call me back? | Potrebbe chiedergli/chiederle di richiamarmi?<br>*Potraybbay keeaydayrlly/keeaydayrlay dee reekeeahmahrmee?* |
| My name's... My number's... | Il mio nome è...Il mio numero è...<br>*Eel meeo nomay ay...Eel meeo noomayro ay...* |
| Could you tell him/her I called? | Gli/le dica che ho chiamato<br>*Lly/lay deekah kay o keeahmahto* |
| I'll call him/her back tomorrow | Lo/la richiamerò domani<br>*Lo/lah reekyahmayro domahnee* |

# Shopping



10

# 10 Shopping

● **Shops** are generally open Monday to Saturday from 9am to 1pm and 3:30 to 7:30pm or 4 to 8pm. Grocery shops may not re-open until 5pm and could stay open until 9pm in the summer. Shops, department stores and supermarkets usually close for a half day during the week - usually Monday morning, Thursday afternoon or Saturday afternoon. This varies from place to place.

alimentari
grocery shop
barbiere
barber's
bigiotteria
costume jewellery
calzature
footwear
calzolaio
cobbler
cartoleria
stationery shop
casalinghi
household goods
copisteria
typing agency
edicola
news-stand
enoteca
stock of vintage wines
erboristeria
herbalist's shop
farmacia
pharmacy
fioraio
florist
forno/fornaio
bakery
fruttivendolo
green grocer
gelateria
icecream shop
gioielleria
jeweller
grande magazzino
department store
istituto di bellezza
beauty salon
latteria
dairy (shop selling dairy products)
lavanderia
laundry
lavanderia a gettone/a secco
coin-operated laundry/dry cleaner
libreria
book shop
macelleria
butcher's shop
riparazione moto/biciclette
motorbike and bicycle repairs
mercato
market
merceria
haberdashery
negozio dell'usato
second-hand shop
negozio di abbigliamento
clothing shop
negozio di articoli da campeggio
camping supplies shop
negozio di articoli di fotografia
camera shop
negozio di articoli sportivi
sporting goods
negozio di biancheria per la casa
household linen shop
negozio di dischi
music shop (CDs, tapes etc)
negozio di elettrodomestici
household appliances (white goods)
negozio di frutta e verdura /fruttivendolo
fruit and vegetable shop
negozio di giocattoli
toy shop
negozio di strumenti musicali
musical instrument shop
negozio fai-da-te
DIY shop
oreficeria
goldsmith
orologeria
watches and clocks
ottico
optician
panetteria
baker's shop
parrucchiere
hairdresser
pasticceria
confectioner's/cake shop
pelletteria
leather goods
pellicceria
furrier
pescivendolo/ pescheria
fishmonger
polleria
poultry shop
profumeria
perfumery
salumeria
delicatessen
supermercato
supermarket
tabacchi
tobacconist
vivaio
nursery (plants)

## 10.1 Shopping conversations

| | |
|---|---|
| Where can I get...? | Dove posso comprare...?<br>*Dovay posso komprahray...?* |
| When is this shop open? | Quando è aperto questo negozio?<br>*Kwahndo ay ahpayrto kwaysto naygotzeeo?* |
| Could you tell me where the...department is? | Mi potrebbe indicare il reparto...?<br>*Mee potraybbay eendeekahray eel raypahrto...?* |
| Could you help me, please? I'm looking for... | Mi potrebbe aiutare? Cerco...<br>*Mee potraybbay aeeootahray? Chayrko...* |
| Do you sell English/ American newspapers? | Vende dei giornali inglesi/americani?<br>*Venday dayee jornahlee eenglaysee/ahmayreekahnee?* |

| | |
|---|---|
| La stanno servendo? | Are you being served? |

| | |
|---|---|
| No, I'd like... | No. Vorrei...<br>*No. Vorrayee...* |
| I'm just looking, if that's all right | Sto solo guardando<br>*Sto solo gwahrdahndo* |

| | |
|---|---|
| (Desidera) altro? | (Would you like) anything else? |

| | |
|---|---|
| Yes, I'd also like... | Sì, mi dia anche...<br>*See, mee deeah ahnkay...* |
| No, thank you. That's all | No grazie, basta così<br>*No grahtzeeay, bahstah cozee* |
| Could you show me...? | Mi potrebbe far vedere...?<br>*Mee potraybbay fahr vaydayray...?* |
| I'd prefer... | Preferisco...<br>*Prayfayreesko...* |
| This is not what I'm looking for | Non è quello che cerco<br>*Non ay kwayllo kay chayrko* |
| Thank you. I'll keep looking | Grazie. Proverò da qualche altra parte<br>*Grahtzeeay. Provayro dah kwahlkay ahltrah pahrtay* |
| Do you have something...? | Ha qualcosa di...?<br>*Ah kwahlkosah dee...?* |
| – less expensive? | Ha qualcosa di meno caro?<br>*Ah kwahlkosah dee mayno kahro?* |
| – smaller? | Ha qualcosa di più piccolo?<br>*Ah kwahlkosah dee peeoo peekkolo?* |
| – larger? | Ha qualcosa di più grande?<br>*Ah kwahlkosah dee peeoo grahnday?* |
| I'll take this one | Prendo questo/a qui<br>*Prayndo kwaysto/ah kwee* |
| Does it come with instructions? | Ci sono le istruzioni per l'uso?<br>*Chee sono lay eestrootzeeonee payr loozo?* |
| It's too expensive | E' troppo caro<br>*Ay troppo kahro* |

| | |
|---|---|
| I'll give you... | Le posso dare...<br>*Lay posso dahray...* |
| Could you keep this for me? I'll come back for it later | Me lo potrebbe tenere da parte? Verrò a prenderlo più tardi<br>*May lo potraybbay taynayray dah pahrtay? Vayrro ah prayndayrlo peeoo tahrdee* |
| Do you have a bag? for me, please? | Ha un sacchetto?<br>*Ah oon sahkkaytto?* |
| Could you giftwrap it, please? | Mi potrebbe fare una confezione regalo, per favore?<br>*Mee potraybbay fahray oonah konfaytzeeonay raygahlo, payr fahvoray?* |

| | |
|---|---|
| Mi dispiace, questo non ce l'abbiamo | I'm sorry, we don't have that. |
| Mi dispiace, sono finiti/e | I'm sorry, we're sold out. |
| Mi dispiace, arriverà solo tra... | I'm sorry, it won't come back in until.... |
| Paghi alla cassa | Please pay at the cash desk |
| Non accettiamo carte di credito | We don't accept credit cards. |
| Non accettiamo traveller cheques | We don't accept traveller's cheques. |
| Non accettiamo valuta straniera | We don't accept foreign currency. |

## 10.2 Food

| | |
|---|---|
| I'd like a hundred grams of..., please | Vorrei un etto di...<br>*Vorrayee oon aytto dee...* |
| I'd like half a kilo/five hundred grams of... | Vorrei mezzo chilo/cinquecento grammi di...<br>*Vorrayee maydzo keelo/cheenkwaychaynto grahmmee dee...* |
| I'd like a kilo of... | Vorrei un chilo di...<br>*Vorrayee oon keelo dee...* |
| Could you...it for me, please? | Me lo potrebbe...?<br>*May lo potraybbay...?* |
| – slice it/cut it up for me, please? | Me lo potrebbe affettare/tagliare a pezzi?<br>*May lo potraybbay ahffayttahray/tahllyahray ah paytzee?* |
| – grate it for me, please? | Me lo potrebbe grattugiare?<br>*May lo potraybbay grahttoojahray?* |
| Can I order it? | Potrei ordinarlo?<br>*Potrayee ordeenahrlo?* |
| I'll pick it up tomorrow/ at... | Verrò a prenderlo domani/alle...<br>*Vayrro ah prayndayrlo domahny/ahllay...* |
| Can you eat/drink this? | Si può mangiare/bere questo?<br>*See pwo mahnjahray/bayhray kwaysto?* |
| What's in it? | Cosa c'è dentro?<br>*Kosah chay dayntro?* |

## 10.3 Clothing and shoes

|  |  |  |
|---|---|---|
| I saw something in the window. Shall I point it out? | Ho visto qualcosa in vetrina. Vuole che glielo indichi? | *O veesto kwahlkosah een vaytreenah. Vwolay kay lyeeaylo eendeekee?* |
| I'd like something to go with this | Vorrei qualcosa che vada bene con questo/a | *Vorrayee kwahlkosah kay vahdah behnay kon kwaysto/ah* |
| Do you have shoes to match this? | Ha delle scarpe nello stesso colore di questo/a? | *Ah dayllay skahrpay nayllo staysso koloray dee kwaysto/ah?* |
| I'm a size...in the UK | In Inghilterra la mia misura è... | *Een Eengeeltayrrah lah meeah meezoorah ay...* |
| Can I try this on? | Posso provarlo/provarla? | *Posso provahrlo/provahrlah?* |
| Where's the fitting room? | Dov'è il camerino? | *Dovay ay eel kahmayreeno?* |
| It doesn't suit me | Non mi sta bene | *Non mee stah bayhnay* |
| This is the right size | Questa è la misura giusta | *Kwaystah ay lah meezoorah joostah* |
| It doesn't look good on me | Mi sta male | *Mee stah mahlay* |
| Do you have this/these in...? | Ha questo(a)/questi(e) in...? | *Ah kwaysto(ah)/kwaystee(ay) een...?* |
| The heel's too high/low | Il tacco è troppo alto/basso | *Eel tahkko ay troppo ahlto/bahsso* |
| Is this real leather? | E' pelle vera? | *Ay payllay vayhrah?* |
| Is this genuine hide? | E' vero cuoio? | *Ay vayhro kwoeeo?* |
| I'm looking for a...for a...year-old child | Cerco un/una...per un bambino/una bambina di...anni | *Chayrko oon/oonah...payr oon bahmbeeno/oonah bahmbeenah dee...ahnnee* |
| I'd like a... | Vorrei un/una...di... | *Vorrayee oon/oonah...dee...* |
| – silk | Vorrei un/una...di seta | *Vorrayee oon/oonah...dee saytah* |
| – cotton | Vorrei un/una...di cotone | *Vorrayee oon/oonah...dee kotonay* |
| – woollen | Vorrei un/una...di lana | *Vorrayee oon/oonah...dee lahnah* |
| – linen | Vorrei un/una...di lino | *Vorrayee oon/oonah...dee leeno* |
| At what temperature should I wash it? | A che temperatura va lavato/a? | *Ah kay taympayrahtoorah vah lahvahto/ah?* |
| Will it shrink in the wash? | Si restringe con il lavaggio? | *See raystreenjay kon eel lahvahdjo?* |

| | | |
|---|---|---|
| Bucato a mano | Lavaggio a secco | Non stirare |
| Hand wash | Dry clean | Do not iron |
| Bucato in lavatrice | Non centrifugare | Stendere piatto |
| Machine washable | Do not spin dry | Lay flat |

***At the cobbler***

Could you mend these shoes? ___ Mi può riparare queste scarpe?
*Mee pwo reepahrahray kwaystay skahrpay?*

Could you resole/reheel these shoes? ___ Potrebbe risuolare queste scarpe/rifare i tacchi a queste scarpe?
*Potraybbay reeswolahray kwaystay skahrpay/reefahray ee tahkkee ah kwaystay skahrpay?*

When will they be ready? ___ Quando saranno pronte?
*Kwahndo sahrahnno prontay?*

I'd like..., please ___ Vorrei...
*Vorrayee...*

– a tin of shoe polish ___ Vorrei una scatola di lucido da scarpe
*Vorrayee oonah skahtolah dee loocheedo dah skahrpay*

– a pair of shoelaces ___ Vorrei un paio di lacci
*Vorrayee oon paheeo dee lahtchee*

## 10.4 Photographs and video

I'd like a film for this camera, please ___ Vorrei una pellicola per questa macchina fotografica
*Vorrayee oonah paylleekolah payr kwaystah mahkkeenah fotograhfeekah*

I'd like a cartridge, please ___ Vorrei una cassetta
*Vorrayee oonah kahssayttah*

– a one twenty-six cartridge ___ Vorrei una cassetta centoventisei
*Vorrayee oonah kahssayttah chayntovaynteesay*

– a slide film ___ Vorrei una pellicola diapositive
*Vorrayee oonah paylleekolah deeahposeeteevay*

– a movie cassette, please ___ Vorrei una cassetta per cinepresa
*Vorrayee oonah kahssayttah payr cheenaypraysah*

– a videotape ___ Vorrei una cassetta per videoregistrazione
*Vorrayee oonah kahssayttah payr veedayo-rayjeestrahtzeeonay*

– colour/black and white ___ – a colori/bianco e nero
*– ah koloree/beeahnko ay nayhro*

– super eight ___ – super otto
*– soopayr otto*

– 12/24/36 exposures ___ – dodici/ventiquattro/trentasei pose
*– dodeechee/vaynteekwahttro/trayntahsayèe posay*

– ASA/DIN number ___ – numero ASA/DIN
*– noomayro ASA/DEEN*

### Problems

| | |
|---|---|
| Could you load the film for me, please? | Potrebbe mettermi il rullino nella macchina fotografica? *Potraybbay mayttayrmee eel roolleeno nellah mahkkeenah fotograhfeekah?* |
| Could you take the film out for me, please? | Potrebbe levare la pellicola dalla macchina fotografica? *Potraybbay layvahray lah paylleekolah dahllah mahkkeenah fotograhfeekah?* |
| Should I replace the batteries? | Devo cambiare le pile? *Dayvo kahmbyahray lay peelay?* |
| Could you have a look at my camera, please? It's not working | Potrebbe controllare la mia macchina fotografica? Non funziona più *Potraybbay kontrollahray lah meeah mahkkeenah fotograhfeekah? Non foontzeeonah peeoo* |
| The...is broken | ....è guasto/a *....ay gwahsto/ah* |
| The film's jammed | La pellicola si è bloccata *Lah paylleekolah see ay blokkahtah* |
| The film's broken | La pellicola si è rotta *Lah paylleekolah see ay rottah* |
| The flash isn't working | Il flash non funziona *Eel flash non foontzeeonah* |

### Processing and prints

| | |
|---|---|
| I'd like to have this film developed/printed, please | Vorrei far sviluppare/far stampare questa pellicola *Vorrayee fahr sveelooppahray/fahr stahmpahray kwaystah paylleekolah* |
| I'd like...prints from each negative | Vorrei...copie di ogni negativo *Vorrayee...copeeay dee onyee naygahteevo* |
| glossy/mat | lucido/opaco *loocheedo/opahko* |
| 6x9 | sei per nove *sayee payr novay* |
| I'd like to order reprints of these photos | Vorrei far fare un'altra ristampa di queste foto *Vorrayee fahr fahray oonahltrah reestahmpah dee kwaystay foto* |
| I'd like to have this photo enlarged | Vorrei far ingrandire questa foto *Vorrayee fahr eengrahndeeray kwaystah foto* |
| How much is processing? | Quanto costa lo sviluppo? *Kwahnto kostah lo sveelooppo?* |
| How much for printing? | Quanto costa la stampa? *Kwahnto kostah lah stahmpah?* |
| How much is are the reprints? | Quanto costa la ristampa? *Kwahnto kostah lah reestahmpah?* |
| How much is it for enlargement? | Quanto costa l'ingrandimento? *Kwahnto kostah leengrahndeemaynto?* |
| When will they be ready? | Quando saranno pronte? *Kwahndo sahrahnno prontay?* |

## .5 At the hairdresser's

|  |  |  |
| --- | --- | --- |
| Do I have to make an appointment? | Bisogna prendere un appuntamento? | *Beezoneeah prayndayray oon ahppoontahmaynto?* |
| Can I come in straight away? | E' subito a mia disposizione? | *Ay soobeeto ah meeah deesposeetzeeonay?* |
| How long will I have to wait? | Quanto devo aspettare? | *Kwahnto dayvo ahspayttahray?* |
| I'd like a shampoo/ haircut | Vorrei farmi lavare/tagliare i capelli | *Vorrayèe fahrmee lahvahray/tahllyahray ee kahpayllee* |
| I'd like a shampoo for oily/dry hair, please | Vorrei uno shampoo per capelli grassi/secchi | *Vorrayee oono shahmpo payr kahpayllee grahssy/saykkee* |
| I'd like an anti-dandruff shampoo | Vorrei uno shampoo anti-forfora | *Vorrayee oono shahmpo ahnteeforforah* |
| I'd like a colour-rinse shampoo, please | Vorrei uno shampoo colorante | *Vorrayee oono shahmpo kolorahntay* |
| I'd like a shampoo with conditioner, please | Vorrei uno shampoo con balsamo | *Vorrayee oono shahmpo kon bahlsahmo* |
| I'd like highlights, please | Vorrei i colpi di sole | *Vorrayee ee kolpee dee solay* |
| Do you have a colour chart, please? | Ha una tabella dei colori, per favore? | *Ah oonah tahbayllah dayèe koloree, payr fahvoray?* |
| I'd like to keep the same colour | Non vorrei cambiare colore | *Non vorrayee kahmbeeahray koloray* |
| I'd like it darker/lighter | Li vorrei più scuri/più chiari | *Lee vorrayee peeoo skooree/peeoo keeahree* |
| I'd like/I don't want hairspray | Vorrei/Non voglio la lacca | *Vorrayee/Non vollyo lah lahkkah* |
| – gel | – il gel | *– eel jayl* |
| – lotion | – la lozione | *– lah lotzeeonay* |
| I'd like a short fringe | Vorrei una frangetta corta | *Vorrayee oonah frahnjayttah kortah* |
| Not too short at the back | Non troppo corti dietro | *Non troppo kortee deeayhtro* |
| Not too long | Non troppo lunghi | *Non troppo loongee* |
| I'd like it curly/not too curly | Li vorrei ricci/non troppo ricci | *Lee vorrayee reetchee/non troppo reetchee* |
| It needs a little/ a lot taken off | Me li tagli un po' più corti/molto più corti | *May lee tahlly oon po peeoo kortee/molto peeoo kortee* |
| I'd like a completely different style/a different cut | Vorrei cambiare pettinatura/un taglio diverso | *Vorrayee kahmbyahray paytteenahtoorah/oon tahleeo deevayrso* |
| I'd like it the same as in this photo | Vorrei un taglio come in questa foto | *Vorrayèe oon tahllyo komay een kwaystah foto* |

| | |
|---|---|
| – as that lady's | – come quella signora<br>*– komay kwayllah seeneeorah* |
| Could you put the drier up/down a bit? | Può alzare/abbassare un po'il casco?<br>*Pwo ahltzahray/ahbbahssahray oon po eel kahsko?* |
| I'd like a facial | Vorrei una maschera per il viso<br>*Vorrayee oonah mahskayhra payr eel veezo* |

| | |
|---|---|
| Come desidera che siano tagliati i capelli? | How do you want it cut? |
| Quale taglio ha in mente? | What style did you have in mind? |
| Quale colore desidera? | What colour did you want it? |
| Le va bene la temperatura? | Is the temperature all right for you? |
| Desidera leggere qualcosa? | Would you like something to read? |
| Desidera bere qualcosa? | Would you like a drink? |
| Le va bene così? | Is this what you had in mind? |

| | |
|---|---|
| – a manicure | la manicure<br>*– lah mahneekooray* |
| – a massage | – un massaggio<br>*– oon mahssahdjo* |
| Could you trim my..., please? | Vorrei che mi desse una spuntatina<br>*Vorrayee kay mee dayssay oonah spoontahteenah* |
| – fringe? | – alla frangetta<br>*– ahllah frahnjayttah* |
| – beard? | – alla barba<br>*– ahllah bahrbah* |
| – moustache? | – ai baffi<br>*– ahee bahffee* |
| I'd like a shave, please | Mi faccia la barba, per favore<br>*Mee fahtchah lah bahrbah, payr fahvoray* |
| I'd like a wet shave, please | Vorrei essere raso con la lametta<br>*Vorray ayssayray rahzo kon lah lahmayttah* |

# At the Tourist Information Centre

# At the Tourist Information Centre

## 11.1 Places of interest

● **There are three main categories** of tourist office: regional, provincial and local. Regional offices are mainly concerned with planning and budgeting etc. Provincial offices (EPT or APT) usually have information on regions and towns. A good range of more specific local information about buses, museums, tours etc. is available at CIT and AAST offices. Tourist offices are generally open Monday to Friday, 8:30am to 12 or 1pm and 3pm to 7pm. Some also open on Saturdays and Sundays during the summer.

| | |
|---|---|
| Where's the Tourist Information, please? | Senta, dov'è l'ufficio informazioni turistiche?<br>*Sayntah, dovay ay looffeetcheeo eenformahtzeeonee tooreesteekay?* |
| Do you have a city map? | Ha una piantina della città, per favore?<br>*Ah oonah peeahnteenah dayllah cheettah, pahr fahvoray?* |
| Where is the museum? | Dov`è il museo?<br>*Dovay ay eel moosayo?* |
| Where can I find a church? | Dove posso trovare una chiesa?<br>*Dovay posso trovahray oonah keeaysah?* |
| Could you give me some information about...? | Mi potrebbe dare qualche informazione su...?<br>*Mee potraybbay dahray kwahlkay eenformahtzeeonay soo...?* |
| How much is this? | Quanto costa?<br>*Kwahnto kostah?* |
| What are the main places of interest? | Quali sono i monumenti più interessanti da vedere?<br>*Kwahlee sono ee monoomayntee peeoo eentayrayssahntee dah vaydayray?* |
| Could you point them out on the map? | Me li potrebbe indicare sulla pianta?<br>*May lee potraybbay eendeekahray soollah pyahntah?* |
| What do you recommend? | Cosa ci consiglia?<br>*Kosah chee konseellyah?* |
| We'll be here for a few hours | Ci fermeremo qui per qualche ora<br>*Chee fayrmayraymo kwee payr kwahlkay orah* |
| We'll be here for a day | Ci fermeremo qui per un giorno<br>*Chee fayrmayraymo kwee payr oon jorno* |
| We'll be here for a week | Ci fermeremo qui per una settimana<br>*Chee fayrmayraymo kwee payr oonah saytteemahnah* |
| We're interested in... | Siamo interessati a...<br>*Seeahmo eentayhrayssahtee ah...* |
| Is there a scenic walk around the city? | E' possibile seguire un itinerario turistico della città?<br>*Ay posseebeelay saygweeray oon eeteenayrahreeo tooreesteeko dayllah cheettah?* |
| How long does it take? | Quanto dura?<br>*Kwahnto doorah?* |

| | |
|---|---|
| Where does it start/end? | Dove comincia/finisce?<br>*Dovay komeenchah/feeneeshay?* |
| Are there any boat trips? | E' possibile fare un giro in battello?<br>*Ay posseebeelay fahray oon jeero een bahttayllo?* |
| Where can we board? | Dove possiamo imbarcarci?<br>*Dovay posseeahmo eembahrkahrchee?* |
| Are there any coach tours? | E' possibile fare un giro della città in pullman?<br>*Ay posseebeelay fahray oon jeero dayllah cheettah een poollmahn?* |
| Where do we get on? | Dove possiamo salire?<br>*Dovay posseeahmo sahleeray?* |
| Is there a guide who speaks English? | C'è una guida che parla inglese?<br>*Chay oonah gweedah kay pahrla englaysay?* |
| What trips can we take around the area? | Quali gite si possono fare nei dintorni?<br>*Kwahlee jeetay see possono fahray nayee deentornee?* |
| Are there any excursions? | Ci sono delle escursioni?<br>*Chee sono dayllay ayskoorseeonee?* |
| Where do they go? | Dove vanno?<br>*Dovay vahnno?* |
| We'd like to go to... | Vogliamo andare a...<br>*Vollyahmo ahndahray ah...* |
| How long is the excursion? | Quanto tempo dura l'escursione?<br>*Kwahnto taympo doorah layskoorseeonay?* |
| How long do we stay in...? | Per quanto tempo ci fermeremo a...?<br>*Payr kwahnto taympo chee fayrmayraymo ah...?* |
| Are there any guided tours? | Ci sono delle visite guidate?<br>*Chee sono dayllay veeseetay gweedahtay?* |
| How much free time will we have there? | Quanto tempo libero avremo a disposizione?<br>*Kwahnto taympo leebayro ahvraymo ah deesposeetzeeonay?* |
| We want to have a walk around/to go on foot | Vogliamo fare un giro a piedi<br>*Vollyahmo fahray oon jeero ah peeaydee* |
| Can we hire a guide? | E' possibile avere una guida?<br>*Ay posseebeelay ahvayray oonah gweedah?* |
| Can we book an alpine hut? | E' possibile prenotare dei rifugi alpini?<br>*Ay poosseebeelay praynotahray dayee reefoojee ahlpeenee?* |
| What time does... open/close? | A che ora apre/chiude...?<br>*Ah kay orah ahpray/keeooday...?* |
| What days is...open/ closed? | Quali sono i giorni in cui...è aperto/a/chiuso/a?<br>*Kwahlee sono ee jornee een kooee...ay ahpayrto/ah keeoozo/ah?* |
| What's the admission price? | Quanto costa un biglietto d'ingresso?<br>*Kwahnto kostah oon beellyaytto deengraysso?* |
| Is there a group discount? | C'è uno sconto per gruppi?<br>*Chay oono skonto payr grooppee?* |
| Is there a child discount? | C'è uno sconto per bambini?<br>*Chay oono skonto payr bahmbeenee?* |

| | |
|---|---|
| Is there a discount for pensioners/senior citizens? | C'è uno sconto per anziani?<br>*Chay oono skonto payr ahntzeeahnee?* |
| Can I take (flash) photos/can I film here? | Qui è permesso fotografare (con il flash)/filmare?<br>*Kwee ay payrmaysso fotograhfahray (kon eel flash)/feelmahray?* |
| Do you have any postcards of...? | Avete cartoline di...?<br>*Avaytay kahrtoleenay dee...?* |
| Do you have an English...? | Ha un/una...in inglese?<br>*Ah oon/oonah...een eenglaysay?* |
| – catalogue? | – catalogo?<br>*– kahtahlogo?* |
| – programme? | – programma?<br>*– prograhmmah?* |
| – brochure? | – opuscolo?<br>*– opooskolo?* |

## 11.2 Going out

● **The main theatre season** is during the winter. Classical music concerts are performed throughout the year. Florence offers the *Maggio Musicale Fiorentino*, *La Scala* is Milan's famous opera house and *Umbria Jazz* takes place in *Perugia* in July. There is a very popular Italian film industry and most foreign films are dubbed into Italian. Venice offers an international film festival and the *Biennale*, a visual arts festival held every two years.

| | |
|---|---|
| Do you have this week's/month's entertainment guide? | Ha il calendario delle manifestazioni e degli spettacoli di questa settimana/di questo mese?<br>*Ah eel kahlayndahreeo dayllay mahneefaystatzeeonee ay daylly spayttahkkolee dee kwaystah saytteemahnah/dee kwaysto maysay?* |
| What's on tonight? | Che spettacoli ci sono stasera?<br>*Kay spayttahkolee chee sono stahsayhrah?* |
| We want to go to... | Vorremmo andare a...<br>*Vorraymmo ahndahray ah...* |
| What's on at the cinema? | Che film danno al cinema?<br>*Kay feelm dahnno ahl cheenaymah?* |
| What sort of film is that? | Che tipo di film è?<br>*Kay teepo dee feelm ay?* |
| – suitable for everyone | – per tutti<br>*– payr toottee* |
| – not suitable for under 12s/under 16s | – vietato ai minori di dodici/sedici anni<br>*– veeaytahto ayee meenoree dee dodeechee/saydeechee ahnnee* |
| – original version | – versione originale<br>*– vayrseeonay oreejeenahlay* |
| – subtitled | – con sottotitoli<br>*– kon sottoteetolee* |
| – dubbed | – doppiato<br>*– doppeeahto* |
| Is it a continuous showing? | E' uno spettacolo continuato?<br>*Ay oono spayttahkolo konteenooahto?* |

| | |
|---|---|
| What's on at...? | Che danno a...?<br>*Kay dahnno ah...?* |
| – the theatre? | – al teatro?<br>*– ahl tayahtro?* |
| – the opera? | – al teatro lirico?<br>*– ahl tayahtro leereeko?* |
| What's happening in the concert hall? | Quale concerto danno al teatro?<br>*Kwahlay konchayrto dahnno ahl tayahtro?* |
| Where can I find a good disco around here? | C'è una buona discoteca qui vicino?<br>*Chay oonah bwonah deeskotaykah kwee veecheeno?* |
| Is it members only? | E' richiesta la tessera?<br>*Ay reekeeaystah lah tayssayrah?* |
| Where can I find a good nightclub around here? | C'è un buon night qui vicino?<br>*Chay oon bwon neeght kwee veecheeno?* |
| Is it evening wear only? | E' obbligatorio l'abito da sera?<br>*Ay obbleegahtoreeo lahbeeto dah sayhrah?* |
| Should I/we dress up? | E' necessario un abito elegante?<br>*Ay naychayssahreeo oon ahbeeto aylaygahntay?* |
| What time does the show start? | A che ora comincia lo show?<br>*Ah kay orah komeenchah lo show?* |
| When's the next soccer match? | Quando è la prossima partita di calcio?<br>*Kwahndo ay lah prosseemah pahrteetah dee kahlcho?* |
| Who's playing? | Chi gioca?<br>*Kee jokah?* |
| I'd like an escort (m/f) for tonight | Stasera vorrei un accompagnatore/un'accompagnatrice<br>*Stahsayhrah vorrayèe oon ahkkompahneeahtroray/ oonahkkompahneeatreechay* |

## 11.3 Booking tickets

| | |
|---|---|
| Could you book some tickets for us? | Ci potrebbe fare la prenotazione, per favore?<br>*Chee potraybbay fahray lah praynotatzeeonay payr fahvoray?* |
| We'd like to book... seats/a table for... | Vogliamo...posti/un tavolo per...<br>*Vollyahmo...postee/oon tahvolo payr...* |
| – seats in the stalls in the main section | Vogliamo...poltrone in platea in sala<br>*Vollyahmo...poltronay een plahtayah een sahlah* |
| – seats in the circle | Vogliamo...posti in galleria<br>*Vollyahmo...postee een gahllayryah* |
| – a box for... | Vogliamo un palco con...posti<br>*Vollyahmo oon pahlko kon...postee* |
| – front row seats/a table for...at the front | Vogliamo...posti/un tavolo per...nelle prime file<br>*Vollyahmo...postee/oon tahvolo payr...nayllay preemay feelay* |
| ...seats in the middle/a table in the middle | Vogliamo...posti/un tavolo al centro<br>*Vollyahmo...postee/oon tahvolo ahl chayntro* |
| ...back row seats/a table at the back | Vogliamo...posti/un tavolo in fondo<br>*Vollyahmo...postee/oon tahvolo een fondo* |

| | |
|---|---|
| Could I book...seats for the...o'clock performance? | E' possibile prenotare...posti per lo spettacolo delle...?<br>*Ay posseebeelay praynotahray...postee payr lo spayttahkolo dayllay...?* |
| Are there any seats left for tonight? | Ci sono ancora biglietti per stasera?<br>*Chee sono ahnkorah beellyayttee payr stahsayhrah?* |
| How much is a ticket? | Quanto costa un biglietto?<br>*Kwahnto kostah oon beellyaytto?* |
| When can I pick up the tickets? | Quando posso ritirare i biglietti?<br>*Kwahndo posso reeteerahray ee beellyayttee?* |
| I've got a reservation | Ho prenotato<br>*O praynotahto* |
| My name's... | Il mio nome è...<br>*eel meeo nomay ay...* |

| | |
|---|---|
| Per quale spettacolo vuole fare una prenotazione? | Which performance do you want to book for? |
| Che tipo di posto? | Where would you like to sit? |
| E' tutto esaurito | Everything's sold out |
| Sono rimasti solo posti in piedi | It's standing room only |
| Sono rimasti solo posti in galleria | We've only got circle seats left |
| Sono rimasti solo posti in loggione | We've only got upper circle (in the gods) seats left |
| Sono rimaste solo le poltrone in platea | We've only got stalls seats left |
| Sono rimasti solo posti nelle prime file | We've only got front row seats left |
| Sono rimasti solo i posti in fondo | We've only got seats left at the back |
| Quanti posti desidera? | How many seats would you like? |
| Deve ritirare i biglietti prima delle... | You'll have to pick up the tickets before...o'clock |
| Biglietti prego | Tickets, please |
| Ecco il suo posto | This is your seat |
| Siete seduti nel posto sbagliato | You are in the wrong seat |

# 12 Sports

# 12 Sports

## 12.1 Sporting questions

| | |
|---|---|
| Where can we... around here? | Dove possiamo...qui vicino?<br>*Dovay posseeahmo...kwee veecheeno?* |
| Can I/we hire a...? | E' possibile prendere a nolo un/una...?<br>*Ay posseebeelay praydayray ah nolo oon/oonah...?* |
| Can I/we take...lessons? | E' possibile prendere lezioni di...?<br>*Ay posseebeelay prendayray laytzeeonee dee...?* |
| How much is that per hour/per day/How much is each one? | Quanto costa all'ora/al giorno/a lezione?<br>*Kwahnto kostah ahllorah/ahl jorno/ah laytzeeonay?* |
| Do you need a permit for that? | Bisogna avere una licenza?<br>*Beezoneeah ahvayray oonah leechaynzah?* |
| Where can I get the permit? | Dove posso ottenere questa licenza?<br>*Dovay posso ottaynayray kwaystah leechaynzah?* |

## 12.2 By the waterfront

| | |
|---|---|
| Is it far (to walk) to the sea? | Per andare al mare, c'è molto (a piedi)?<br>*Payr ahndahray ahl mahray chay molto (ah peeaydee)?* |
| Is there a...around here? | C'è un/una...qui vicino?<br>*Chay oon/oonah...kwee veecheeno?* |
| – a swimming pool | C'è una piscina?<br>*Chay oonah peesheenah?* |
| – a sandy beach | C'è una spiaggia di sabbia?<br>*Chay oonah speeahdjah dee sahbbeeah?* |
| – a nudist beach | C'è una spiaggia per nudisti?<br>*Chay oonah speeahdjah payr noodeestee?* |
| – mooring (place)/dock | C'è un molo d'attracco?<br>*Chay oon molo dahttrahkko?* |
| Are there any rocks here? | Ci sono degli scogli qui?<br>*Chee sono daylly skolly kwee?* |
| When's high/low tide? | Quando c'è l'alta marea/la bassa marea?<br>*Kwahndo chay lahltah mahrayah/lah bahssah mahrayah?* |
| What's the water temperature? | Qual è la temperatura dell'acqua?<br>*Kwahlay ay lah taympayrahtoorah dayllahkwah?* |
| Is it (very) deep here? | E' (molto) profondo qui?<br>*Ay (molto) profondo kwee?* |
| Is it safe (for children) to swim here? | E' sicuro (per i bambini) fare il bagno qui?<br>*Ay seekooro (payr ee bahmbeenee) fahray eel bahneeo kwee?* |
| Are there any currents? | Ci sono correnti?<br>*Chee sono korrayntee?* |
| Are there any rapids/ waterfalls along this river? | Questo fiume ha delle rapide/delle cascate?<br>*Kwaysto feeoomay ah dayllay rahpeeday/kahskahtay?* |

| | |
|---|---|
| What does that flag/ buoy mean? | Cosa significa quella bandiera/quella boa? *Kosah seeneefeekah kwayllah bahndeeayrah/kwayllah boah?* |
| Is there a lifeguard on duty? | C'è un bagnino che sorveglia? *Chay oon bahneeno kay sorvellyah?* |
| Are dogs allowed here? | Sono permessi i cani? *Sono payrmayssee ee kahnee?* |
| Is camping on the beach allowed? | E' permesso fare il campeggio sulla spiaggia? *Ay payrmaysso fahray eel kahmpaydjo soollah speeahdjah?* |
| Can we light a fire? | E' permesso fare un fuoco? *Ay payrmaysso fahray oon fwoko?* |

| | | |
|---|---|---|
| Zona di pesca<br>**Fishing waters** | Solo con licenza<br>**Permits only** | Divieto di surfing<br>**No surfing** |
| Pericolo<br>**Danger** | Divieto di balneazione<br>**No swimming** | Pesca vietata<br>**No fishing** |

## 12.3 In the snow

| | |
|---|---|
| Can I take ski lessons here? | E' possibile prendere delle lezioni di sci? *Ay posseebeelay prayndayray dayllay laytzeeonee dee shee?* |
| For beginners/ intermediates | Per principianti/di medio livello *Payr preencheepeeahntee/dee maydeeo leevello* |
| How large are the groups? | Quanti persone ci sono in un gruppo? *Kwahntay payrsonay chee sono een oon grooppo?* |
| What languages are the classes in? | In che lingua fanno lezione? *Een kay leengwah fahnno laytzeeonay?* |
| I'd like a lift pass, please | Vorrei uno skipass *Vorrayee oono skeepahss* |
| Where are the nursery slopes? | Dove sono le piste per i principianti? *Dovay sono lay peestay payr ee preencheepeeahntee?* |
| Are there any cross-country ski runs around here? | Ci sono piste di fondo qui vicino? *Chee sono peestay dee fondo kwee veecheeno?* |
| Have the cross-country runs been marked? | Sono indicate le piste di fondo? *Sono eendeekahtay lay peestay dee fondo?* |
| Are the...open? | Sono aperti...i/le? *Sono ahpayrtee...ee/lay?* |
| – the ski lifts...? | Sono aperti gli skilift? *Sono ahpayrtee lly skeeleeft?* |
| – the chair lifts...? | Sono aperte le seggiovie? *Sono ahpayrtee lay sedgeeoveeay* |
| – the runs...? | Sono aperte le piste? *Sono ahpayrtee lay peestay?* |
| – the cross-country runs...? | Sono aperte le piste di fondo? *Sono ahpayrtay lay peestay dee fondo?* |

# 13 Sickness

# 13 Sickness

## 13.1 Call (fetch) the doctor

● **If you become ill** or need emergency treatment, it is better to go to Casualty *(pronto soccorso)* at your nearest hospital.

| | |
|---|---|
| Could you call (fetch) a doctor quickly, please? | Mi chiami presto il medico, per favore<br>*Mee keeahmy praysto eel maydeeko, payr fahvoray* |
| When does the doctor have surgery? | Quando riceve il medico?<br>*Kwahndo reechayvay eel maydeeko?* |
| When can the doctor come? | Quando potrà venire il medico?<br>*Kwahndo potrah vayneeray eel maydeeko?* |
| Could I make an appointment to see the doctor? | Mi potrebbe fissare un appuntamento con il medico?<br>*Mee potraybbay feessahray oon ahppoontahmaynto con eel maydeeko?* |
| I've got an appointment to see the doctor at... o'clock | Ho un appuntamento con il medico alle...<br>*O oon ahppoontahmaynto con eel maydeeko ahllay...* |
| Which doctor/pharmacy is on night/weekend duty? | Quale medico/farmacia è in servizio notturno/in servizio di fine settimana?<br>*Kwahlay maydeeko/fahrmahcheeah ay een sayrveetzeeo nottoorno/een sayrveetzeeo dee feenay saytteemahnah?* |

## 13.2 Patients' ailments

| | |
|---|---|
| I don't feel well | Mi sento male<br>*Mee saynto mahlay* |
| I'm dizzy | Ho il capogiro<br>*O eel kahpojeero* |
| – ill | Sono ammalato/a<br>*Sono ahmmahlahto/ah* |
| I feel sick (nauseous) | Ho la nausea<br>*O lah nahoozayah* |
| I've got a cold | Sono raffreddato/a<br>*Sono rahffrayddahto/ah* |
| It hurts here | Mi fa male qui<br>*Mee fah mahlay kwee* |
| I've been sick (vomited) | Ho vomitato<br>*O vomeetahto* |
| I've got... | Soffro di...<br>*Soffro dee...* |
| I'm running a temperature of...degrees | Ho la febbre...<br>*O lah faybbrayah...* |
| I've been... | Sono stato/a...<br>*Sono stahto/ah...* |
| – stung by a wasp | Sono stato/a punto/a da una vespa<br>*Sono stahto/ah poonto/ah dah oonah vayspah* |
| – stung by an insect | Sono stato/a punto/a da un insetto<br>*Sono stahto/ah poonto/ah dah oon eensaytto* |
| – bitten by a dog | Sono stato/a morso/a da un cane<br>*Sono stahto/ah morso/ah dah oon kahnay* |

| | |
|---|---|
| – stung by a jellyfish | Sono stato/a punto/a da una medusa<br>*Sono stahto/ah poont/ah dah oonah maydoosah* |
| – bitten by a snake | Sono stato/a morso/a da una serpe<br>*Sono stahto/ah morso/ah dah oonah sayrpay* |
| – bitten by an animal | Sono stato/a morso/a da una bestia<br>*Sono stahto/ah morso/ah dah oonah baysteeah* |
| I've cut myself | Mi sono tagliato/a<br>*Mee sono tahllyahto/ah* |
| I've burned myself | Mi sono bruciato/a<br>*Mee sono broocheeahto/ah* |
| I've grazed/scratched myself (m/f) | Mi sono scorticato/a, graffiato/a<br>*Mee sono skorteekahto/ah, graffeeahto/ah* |
| I've had a fall | Sono caduto/a<br>*Sono kahdooto/ah* |
| I've sprained my ankle | Mi sono storto/a la caviglia<br>*Mee sono storto/ah lah kahveellyah* |
| I'd like the morning-after pill | Vorrei la pillola del giorno dopo<br>*Vorrayèe lah peellolah dayl jorno dopo* |

## 13.3 The consultation

| | |
|---|---|
| Quali disturbi ha? | What seems to be the problem? |
| Da quanto tempo ha questi disturbi? | How long have you had these complaints? |
| Ha sofferto già prima di questi disturbi? | Have you had this trouble before? |
| Ha la febbre? Quanti gradi? | Do you have a temperature? What is it? |
| Si spogli per favore | Get undressed, please |
| Si scopra il torace per favore | Strip to the waist, please |
| Può spogliarsi da questa parte | You can undress there |
| Si scopra il braccio sinistro/destro per favore | Roll up your left/right sleeve, please |
| Si sdrai qui, per favore | Lie down here, please |
| Fa male? | Does this hurt? |
| Respiri profondamente | Breathe deeply |
| Apra la bocca | Open your mouth |

***Patients' medical history***

| | |
|---|---|
| I'm a diabetic | Sono diabetico/a<br>*Sono deeahbayhteeko/ah* |
| I have a heart condition | Soffro di disturbi di cuore<br>*Soffro dee deestoorbee dee kworay* |
| I'm an asthmatic | Soffro di asma<br>*Soffro dee ahsmah* |
| I'm allergic to... | Sono allergico/a a...<br>*Sono ahllayrjeeko/ah ah...* |
| I'm...months pregnant | Sono incinta di...mesi<br>*Sono eencheentah dee...maysee* |

| | |
|---|---|
| I'm on a diet | Seguo una dieta<br>*Saygwo oonah deeaytah* |
| I'm on medication/ the pill | Prendo dei farmaci/la pillola contraccettiva<br>*Prayndo dayee fahrmahchee/lah peellolah kontrahchaytteevah* |
| I've had a heart attack once before | Ho avuto già in passato un attacco cardiaco<br>*O ahvooto jah een pahssahto oon ahttahkko kahrdeeahko* |
| I've had a(n)...operation | Mi hanno fatto un'operazione a...<br>*Mee ahnno fahtto oonopayhrahtzeeonay ah...* |
| I've been ill recently | Sono stato/a ammalato/a di recente<br>*Sono stahto/ah ahmmahlahto/ah dee raychayntay* |
| I've got a stomach ulcer | Soffro di un'ulcera gastrica<br>*Soffro dee oonoolchayrah gahstreekah* |
| I've got my period | Ho le mestruazioni<br>*O lay maystrooahtzeeonee* |

***The diagnosis***

| | |
|---|---|
| E' allergico/a a qualcosa? | Do you have any allergies? |
| Sta prendendo altri farmaci? | Are you on any medication? |
| Segue una dieta? | Are you on a diet? |
| E' incinta? | Are you pregnant? |
| E' stato/a vaccinato/a contro il tetano? | Have you had a tetanus injection? |

| | |
|---|---|
| Non è niente di grave | It's nothing serious |
| Ha una frattura al/alla... | Your...is broken |
| Ha una distorsione al/alla... | You've got a sprained... |
| Ha uno strappo al/alla... | You've got a torn... |
| Ha un'infezione | You've got an infection/ some inflammation |
| Ha un'appendicite | You've got appendicitis |
| Ha una bronchite | You've got bronchitis |
| Ha una malattia venerea | You've got a venereal disease |
| Ha l'influenza | You've got the flu |
| Ha avuto un attacco cardiaco | You've had a heart attack |
| Ha un'infezione (virale, batterica) | You've got a (viral/bacterial) infection |
| Ha una polmonite | You've got pneumonia |
| Ha una gastrite/un'ulcera | You've got gastritis/an ulcer |
| Ha uno strappo muscolare | You've pulled a muscle |
| Ha un'infezione vaginale | You've got a vaginal infection |

| | |
|---|---|
| Ha un'intossicazione alimentare | You've got food poisoning |
| Ha un'insolazione | You've got sunstroke |
| E' allergico a... | You're allergic to... |
| E' incinta | You're pregnant |
| Vorrei fare analizzare il Suo sangue/la Sua orina/le Sue feci | I'd like to have your blood/urine/stools tested |
| La ferita deve essere suturata | It needs stitches |
| La indirizzo da uno specialista/all'ospedale | I'm referring you to a specialist/sending you to hospital. |
| Bisogna far fare qualche radiografia | You'll need some x-rays taken |
| Può aspettare un attimo nella sala d'attesa, per favore? | Could you wait in the waiting room, please? |
| Deve essere operato/a | You'll need an operation |

| | |
|---|---|
| Is it contagious? | E' contagioso?<br>*Ay kontahjozo?* |
| How long do I have to stay...? | Per quanto tempo devo rimanere...?<br>*Payr kwahnto taympo dayvo reemahnayray...?* |
| – in bed | – a letto?<br>*– ah laytto?* |
| – in hospital | – all'ospedale?<br>*– ahllospaydahlay?* |
| Do I have to go on a special diet? | Devo seguire una dieta?<br>*Dayvo saygweeray oonah deeaytah?* |
| Am I allowed to travel? | Mi è permesso viaggiare?<br>*Mee ay payrmaysso veeahdjahray?* |
| Can I make another appointment? | Potrei fissare un nuovo appuntamento?<br>*Potrayee feessahray oon nwovo ahppoontahmaynto?* |
| When do I have to come back? | Quando devo ritornare?<br>*Kwahndo dayvo reetornahray?* |
| I'll come back tomorrow | Ritorno domani<br>*Reetorno domahny* |
| How do I take this medicine? | Come devo prendere questa medicina?<br>*Comay dayvo prayndayray kwaystah maydeecheenah?* |

| | |
|---|---|
| Deve ritornare domani/fra...giorni | Come back tomorrow/in...days' time. |



## 13.4 Medication and prescriptions

| | |
|---|---|
| How many capsules/ drops/injections/ spoonfuls/tablets each time? | Quante capsule/gocce/iniezioni/ cucchiaiate/compresse alla volta?<br>*Kwahntay kahpsoolay/gotchay/ eeneeaytzeeonee/kookkeeaheeahtay/ komprayssay ahllah voltah?* |
| How many times a day? | Quante volte al giorno?<br>*Kwahntay voltay ahl jorno?* |

| | |
|---|---|
| I've forgotten my medication<br>At home I take... | Mi sono dimenticato/a le medicine. A casa prendo...<br>*Mee sono deementeekahto/ah lay maydeecheenay. A kahza prayndo...* |
| Could you make out a prescription for me, please? | Mi potrebbe scrivere una ricetta?<br>*Mee potraybbay skreevayray oonah reechayttah?* |

| | |
|---|---|
| Le prescrivo degli antibiotici/uno sciroppo/un tranquillante/degli analgesici | I'm prescribing antibiotics/a mixture/a tranquillizer/pain killers |
| Bisogna che si riposi | Have lots of rest |
| Non può uscire | Stay indoors |
| Non può alzarsi | Stay in bed |

capsule
capsules
compresse
tablets
condurre a termine la cura
finish the course
cucchiaio/cucchiaino
spoonful/teaspoonful
iniezioni
injections
per...giorni
for...days

far sciogliere in acqua
dissolve in water
gocce
drops
inghiottire
swallow (whole)
ogni...ore
every...hours
pomata
ointment
prendere
take

prima di ogni pasto
before meals
queste medicine influiscono sull'abilità di guida
this medication impairs your driving
solo per uso esterno
external use only
spalmare
rub on
...volte al giorno
...times a day

## 13 .5 At the dentist's

| | |
|---|---|
| Do you know a good dentist? | Conosce un buon dentista?<br>*Konoshay oon bwon daynteestah?* |
| Could you make a dentist's appointment for me? It's urgent | Mi potrebbe prendere un appuntamento urgente dal dentista?<br>*Mee potraybbay prayndayray oon ahppoontahmaynto oorjenahtay dahl daynteestah?* |
| Can I come in today, please | Posso venire oggi, per favore?<br>*Posso vayneeray odjee payr fahvoray?* |
| I have a (terrible) toothache | Ho (un) mal di denti (terribile)<br>*O (oon) mahl dee dayntee (tayrreebeelay)* |
| Could you prescribe/ give me a painkiller? | Mi potrebbe prescrivere/dare un analgesico?<br>*Mee potraybbay prayskreevayray/dahray oon ahnahljeezeeko?* |
| I've got a broken tooth | Ho un dente spezzato<br>*O oon dayntay spaytzahto* |
| My filling's come out | Ho perso un'otturazione<br>*O payrso oonottoorahtzeeonay* |
| I've got a broken crown | Si è rotta la capsula<br>*See ay rottah lah kahpsoolah* |

| | |
|---|---|
| I'd like/I don't want a local anaesthetic | Vorrei essere curato/a con/senza anestesia locale<br>*Vorrayee ayssayhray koorahto/ah kon/ saynzah ahnaystayzeeah lokahlay* |
| Could you do a temporary repair? | Mi potrebbe curare adesso in modo provvisorio?<br>*Mee potraybbay koorahray ahdaysso een modo provveezoreeo?* |
| I don't want this tooth pulled | Non voglio un'estrazione<br>*Non vollyo oonaystrahtzeeonay* |
| My denture is broken. Can you fix it? | Ho rotto la dentiera. La può aggiustare?<br>*O rotto lah daynteeayhrah. Lah pwo ahdjoostahray?* |

| | |
|---|---|
| Qual è il dente che Le fa male? | Which tooth hurts? |
| Ha un ascesso | You've got an abscess. |
| Le devo fare una cura canalare | I'll have to do a root canal |
| Le faccio un'anestesia locale | I'm giving you a local anaesthetic |
| Devo estrarre/fare un'otturazione/ limare questo dente | I'll have to pull/fill/file this tooth |
| Devo trapanarlo | I'll have to drill it |
| Apra la bocca | Open wide, please |
| Chiuda la bocca | Close your mouth, please |
| Si sciacqui la bocca | Rinse, please |
| Sente ancora dolore? | Does it hurt still? |

# In trouble

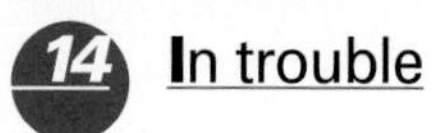

# 14 In trouble

## 14.1 Asking for help

|  |  |
|---|---|
| Help! | Aiuto!<br>*Ayooto!* |
| Fire! | Al fuoco!<br>*Ahl fwoko!* |
| Police! | Polizia!<br>*Poleetzeeah!* |
| Quick/Hurry! | Presto!<br>*Praysto!* |
| Danger! | Pericolo!<br>*Payreekolo!* |
| Watch out! | Attenzione!<br>*Attayntzeeonay!* |
| Stop! | Alt!/Stop!<br>*Ahlt!/Stop!* |
| Be careful!/Go easy! | Attenzione!/Piano!<br>*Attayntzeeonay!/Peeahno!* |
| Get your hands off me! | Giù le mani!<br>*Joo lay mahnee!* |
| Let go! | Lascia!<br>*Lahshah!* |
| Stop thief! | Al ladro!<br>*Ahl lahdro!* |
| Could you help me, please? | Mi potrebbe aiutare?<br>*Mee potraybbay aheeootahray?* |
| Where's the police station/emergency exit/fire escape? | Dov'è la questura/l'uscita di emergenza/la scala di sicurezza?<br>*Dovay ay lah kwaystoorah/loosheetah dee aymayrjayntzah/lah skahlah dee seekooraytzah?* |
| Where's the nearest fire extinguisher? | Dov'è un estintore?<br>*Dovay ay oonaysteentoray?* |
| Call the fire brigade! | Chiami i pompieri!<br>*Keeahmee ee pompeeayhree!* |
| Call the police! | Chiami la polizia!<br>*Keeahmee lah poleetzeeah!* |
| Call an ambulance! | Chiami un'ambulanza!<br>*Keeahmee oonahmboolahntzah!* |
| Where's the nearest phone? | Dov'è un telefono?<br>*Dovay ay oon taylayfono?* |
| Could I use your phone? | Potrei servirmi del Suo telefono?<br>*Potrayee sayrveermee dayl soo-o taylayfono?* |
| What's the emergency number? | Qual è il numero dei servizi di emergenza?<br>*Kwahlay ay eel noomayro dayee sayrveetzee dee aymayrjayntzah?* |
| What's the number for the police? | Qual è il numero della polizia?<br>*Kwahlay ay eel noomayro dayllah poleetzeeah?* |

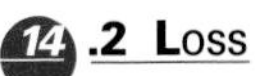

## .2 Loss

| | |
|---|---|
| I've lost my wallet/purse | Ho perso il portafoglio/portamonete<br>*O payrso eel portahfollyo/portahmonaytay* |
| I lost my...here yesterday | Ieri ho dimenticato qui...<br>*Eeayree oh deemayteekahto kwee...* |
| I left my...here | Ho lasciato qui il mio.../la mia...<br>*O lahsheeahto kwee eel meeo.../lah meeah...* |
| Did you find my...? | Ha trovato il mio /la mia...?<br>*Ah trovahto eel meeo /lah meeah...?* |
| It was right here | Stava qui<br>*Stahvah kwee* |
| It's very valuable | E' molto prezioso/a<br>*Ay molto praytzeeozo/ah* |
| Where's the lost property office? | Dov'è l'ufficio oggetti smarriti?<br>*Dovay ay looffeetcheeo odjayttee smahrreetee?* |

## 14.3 Accidents

| | |
|---|---|
| There's been an accident | C'è stato un incidente<br>*Chay stahto ooneencheedayntay* |
| Someone's fallen into the water | Qualcuno è caduto nell'acqua<br>*Kwahlkoono ay kahdooto nayllahkwah* |
| There's a fire | C'è un incendio<br>*Chay ooneenchayndyo* |
| Is anyone hurt? | Ci sono dei feriti?<br>*Chee sono dayee fayhreetee?* |
| (Nobody) someone has been injured | (Non) ci sono dei feriti<br>*(Non) chee sono day fayhreetee* |
| Someone's still trapped inside the car/train | C'è ancora qualcuno intrappolato dentro la macchina/il treno<br>*Chay ahnkorah kwahlkoono eentrahppolahto dayntro lah mahkkeenah/eel trayno* |
| It's not too bad. Don't worry | Non è grave. Non si preoccupi<br>*Non ay grahvay. Non see prayokkoopee* |
| Leave everything the way it is, please | Lasci tutto così com'è, per piacere<br>*Lahshee tootto kozee komay ay, payr peeahchayray* |
| I want to talk to the police first | Vorrei parlare prima alla polizia<br>*Vorrayee pahrlahray preemah ahllah poleetzeeah* |
| I want to take a photo first | Vorrei prima fare una foto<br>*Vorrayee preemah fahray oonah foto* |
| Here's my name and address | Ecco il mio nome e il mio indirizzo<br>*Ekko eel meeo nomay ay eel meeo eendeereetzo* |
| May I have your name and address? | Potrei sapere il Suo nome e il Suo indirizzo?<br>*Potrayee sahpayray eel soo-o nomay ay eel soo-o eendeereetzo?* |
| Could I see your identity card/your insurance papers? | Potrei vedere la Sua carta d'identità/i documenti dell'assicurazione?<br>*Potrayee vaydayray lah sooah kahrtah deedaynteetah/ee dokoomentee dayllasseekoorahtzeeonay?* |

| | |
|---|---|
| Will you act as a witness? | Accetta di testimoniare?<br>*Ahtchayttah dee taysteemoneeahray?* |
| I need this information for insurance purposes | Ho bisogno di questi dati per via dell'assicurazione<br>*O beezoneeo dee kwaystee dahtee payr veeah dayllahsseekoorahtzeeonay* |
| Are you insured? | E' assicurato/a?<br>*Ay ahsseekoorahto/ah?* |
| Third party or comprehensive? | Responsabilità civile o assicurazione completa?<br>*Raysponsahbeeleetah cheeveelay o ahsseekoorahtzeeonay komplaytah?* |
| Could you sign here, please? | Firmi qui, per favore<br>*Feermee kwee, payr fahvoray* |

## 14.4 Theft

| | |
|---|---|
| I've been robbed | Sono stato/a derubato/a<br>*Sono stahto/ah dayroobahto/ah* |
| My...has been stolen | Hanno rubato il mio.../la mia...<br>*Ahnno roobahto eel meeo.../lah meeah...* |
| My car's been broken into | Mi hanno forzato la macchina<br>*Mee ahnno fortzahto la mahkkeenah* |

## 14.5 Missing person

| | |
|---|---|
| I've lost my child/ grandmother | Ho perso mio figlio/mia figlia/mia nonna<br>*O payrso meeo feellyo/meeah feellyah/ meeah nonnah* |
| Could you help me find him/her? | Mi potrebbe aiutare a cercarlo/cercarla?<br>*Mee potraybbay aheeootahray ah chayrkahrlo/chayrkahrlah?* |
| Have you seen a small child? | Ha visto un bambino/una bambina?<br>*Ah veesto oon bahmbeeno/oonah bahmbeenah?* |
| He's/she's...years old | Ha...anni<br>*Ah...annee* |
| He/she's got...hair | Ha i capelli...<br>*Ah ee kahpayllee...* |
| short/long/blond/red/ brown/black/grey/curly/ straight/ frizzy | corti/lunghi/biondi/rossi/bruni/neri/grigi/ ricci/lisci/crespi<br>*kortee/loongee/beeondee/rossee/broonee/ nayree/ greejee/reetchee/krayspee* |
| – a ponytail | – con la coda di cavallo<br>*– kon lah kodah dee kahvahllo* |
| – plaits | – con le trecce<br>*– kon llay traytchay* |
| – a bun | – con una crocchia<br>*– kon loonah crokkeeah* |
| He's/she's got blue/brown/green eyes | Ha gli occhi azzurri/bruni/verdi<br>*Ah lly okkee ahdzoorree/broonee/vayrdee* |
| He/she's wearing swimming trunks/hiking boots | Porta un costume da bagno/gli scarponi<br>*Portah oon kostoomay dah bahneeo/lly skahrponee* |
| with/without glasses, carrying/not carrying a bag | con/senza occhiali, (non) porta una borsa<br>*kon/saynzah okkeeahlee, (non) portah oonah borsah* |

| | |
|---|---|
| He/She is tall/short | È alto/a, basso/a<br>*Ay ahlto/ah, bahsso/ah* |
| This is a photo of him/her | Ecco una sua foto<br>*Ekko oonah sooah foto* |
| He/she must be lost | Deve essersi perso/a<br>*Dayvay ayssayrsee payrso/ah* |

## 14.6 The police

***An arrest***

| | |
|---|---|
| Documenti prego | Your (vehicle) documents, please |
| Ha superato il limite di velocità | You were speeding |
| E' vietato parcheggiare qui | You're not allowed to park here |
| Non ha messo soldi nel parcometro/ parchimetro | You haven't put money in the 'Pay and display'/ parking meter |
| I fari della sua macchina non funzionano | Your lights aren't working |
| Le devo fare una multa di.... | That's a L.....fine |
| Paga direttamente? | Do you want to pay on the spot? |
| Deve pagare subito | You'll have to pay on the spot |

| | |
|---|---|
| I don't speak Italian | Non parlo l'italiano<br>*Non pahrlo leetahleeahno* |
| I didn't see the sign | Non ho visto quel cartello<br>*Non o veesto kwayl kahrtayllo* |
| I don't understand what it says | Non capisco cosa c'è scritto<br>*Non kahpeesko kosah chay skreetto* |
| I was only doing... kilometres an hour | Andavo soltanto a...chilometri all'ora<br>*Ahndahvo soltahnto ah...keelomaytree ahllorah* |
| I'll have my car checked | Farò controllare la macchina<br>*Fahro kontrollahray lah mahkkeenah* |
| I was blinded by oncoming lights | Sono stato/a abbagliato/a<br>*Sono stahto/ah ahbbahllyahto/ah* |

| | |
|---|---|
| Dov'è successo? | Where did it happen? |
| Cosa ha perso? | What's missing? |
| Cosa hanno rubato? | What's been taken? |
| Potrei avere la Sua carta d'identità? | Could I see your identity card/some identification? |
| A che ora è successo? | What time did it happen? |
| Ci sono dei testimoni? | Are there any witnesses? |
| Firmi qui, per favore | Sign here, please |
| Desidera un interprete? | Do you want an interpreter? |

***At the police station***

| | |
|---|---|
| I want to report a collision/missing person/rape | Vorrei denunciare uno scontro/uno smarrimento/uno stupro<br>*Vorrayee daynooncheeahray oono skontro/ oono zmahrreemaynto/oono stoopro* |
| Could you make a statement, please? | Può fare una dichiarazione scritta, per favore?<br>*Pwo fahray oonah deekeeahrahtzeeonay skreettah, payr fahvoray?* |
| Could I have a copy for the insurance? | Mi dia una copia per l'assicurazione<br>*Mee deeah oonah kopeeah payr lahsseekoorahtzeeonay* |
| I've lost everything | Ho perso tutto<br>*O payrso tootto* |
| I've no money left, I'm desperate | Non ho più soldi, sono disperato/a<br>*Non o peeoo soldee, sono deespayrahto/ah* |
| Could you lend me a little money? | Mi potrebbe prestare qualcosa?<br>*Mee potraybbay praystahray kwahlkosah?* |
| I'd like an interpreter | Vorrei un interprete<br>*Vorrayee ooneentayrprayhtay* |
| I'm innocent | Sono innocente<br>*Sono eennochayntay* |
| I don't know anything about it | Non ne so niente<br>*Non nay so neeayntay* |
| I want to speak to someone from the British/ American/ Australian embassy | Vorrei parlare con qualcuno dell'ambasciata Britannica/Americana/ Australiana<br>*Vorrayee pahrlahray con kwahlkoono dayllahmbahshahtah Breetahnneekah/ Ahmayreekahnah/Ahoostrahleeahnah* |
| I want a lawyer who speaks... | Vorrei un avvocato che parli...<br>*Vorrayee oonahvvokahto kay pahrlee...* |

# 15

# Word list

# Word list English - Italian

● **The following word list** is meant to supplement the chapters in this book. Verbs are indicated by the word "verb" and where the gender of a noun is not clear, the word is followed by (m) or (f).

Some of the words not contained in this list can be found elsewhere in the book, eg. alongside the diagrams of the car, bicycle and camping equipment. Many food items can be found in the Italian-English list in chapter 4.7

## A

| | | |
|---|---|---|
| about | circa | *cheerkah* |
| above, up | sopra | *soprah* |
| abroad | all'estero | *ahllaystayro* |
| accident | incidente (m) | *eencheedayntay* |
| adder | vipera | *veepayrah* |
| address | indirizzo | *eendeereetzo* |
| admission | ingresso | *eengraysso* |
| admission price | prezzo del biglietto | *praytzo dayl beellyaytto* |
| advice | consiglio | *konseellyo* |
| after | dopo | *dopo* |
| afternoon | pomeriggio | *pomayreedjo* |
| aftershave | il dopobarba | *eel dopobahrbah* |
| again | di nuovo | *dee nwovo* |
| against | contro | *kontro* |
| age | età | *aytah* |
| Aids | Aids (m) | *ayeeds* |
| air conditioning | aria condizionata | *ahreeah kondeetzeeonahtah* |
| air sickness bag | busta per vomitare | *boostah payr vomeetahray* |
| aircraft | aeroplano | *ahayroplahno* |
| airport | aeroporto | *ahayroporto* |
| alarm | allarme (m) | *ahllahrmay* |
| alarm clock | sveglia | *svayllyah* |
| alcohol | le bevande alcoliche | *lay bayvahnday ahlkoleekay* |
| all the time | di continuo | *dee konteenoo-o* |
| allergic | allergico | *ahllayrjeeko* |
| alone | solo | *solo* |
| always | sempre | *saympray* |
| ambulance | ambulanza | *ahmboolahntzah* |
| amount | somma | *sommah* |
| amusement park | il 'luna' park | *eel 'loonah' pahrk* |
| anaesthetize (verb) | anestetizzare | *ahnaystayteetzahray* |
| anchovy | acciuga | *ahtchoogah* |
| angry | arrabbiato | *ahrrahbbeeahto* |
| animal | animale (m) | *ahneemahlay* |
| ankle | caviglia | *kahveellyah* |
| answer | risposta | *reespostah* |
| ant | formica | *formeekah* |
| anti-diarrhhoea tablets | medicina astringente | *maydeecheenah ahstreenjayntay* |

| | | |
|---|---|---|
| antibiotics | gli antibiotici | *lly ahnteebeeoteechee* |
| antifreeze | antigelo | *ahnteejaylo* |
| antique | antico | *ahnteeko* |
| antiques | gli oggetti antichi | *lly odjayttee ahnteekee* |
| anus | ano | *ahno* |
| apartment | appartamento | *ahppahrtahmaynto* |
| aperitif | aperitivo | *ahpayreeteevo* |
| apple | mela | *maylah* |
| apple juice | succo di mela | *sookko dee maylah* |
| apple pie | torta di mele | *tortah dee maylay* |
| apple sauce | passato di mele | *pahssahto dee maylay* |
| appointment | appuntamento | *ahppoontahmaynto* |
| apricot | albicocca | *ahlbeekokkah* |
| April | aprile (m) | *ahpreellay* |
| architecture | architettura | *ahrkeetayttoorah* |
| area | i dintorni | *ee deentornee* |
| arm | braccio | *brahtcheeo* |
| arrive (verb) | arrivare | *ahrreevahray* |
| arrow | freccia | *fraytchah* |
| art | arte (f) | *ahrtay* |
| artery | arteria | *ahrtayreeah* |
| artichokes | i carciofi | *ee kahrchofee* |
| article | articolo | *ahrteekolo* |
| artificial respiration | la respirazione artificiale | *lah rayspeerahtzeeonay ahrteefeechahlay* |
| arts and crafts | artigianato | *ahrteejahnahto* |
| ashtray | il portacenere | *eel portahchaynayray* |
| ask (verb) | chiedere | *keeaydayray* |
| asparagus | gli asparagi | *lly ahspahrahjee* |
| aspirin | aspirina | *ahspeereenah* |
| assault | la violazione | *lah veeolahtzeeonay* |
| at home | a casa | *ah kahsah* |
| at night | la/di notte | *lah/dee nottay* |
| at the back | in fondo | *een fondo* |
| at the end/at the rear | in fondo | *een fondo* |
| at the front (theatre etc) | nelle prime file | *nayllay preemay feellay* |
| at the front | di fronte | *dee frontay* |
| at the latest | al massimo/al più tardi | *ahl mahsseemo/ ahl peeoo tahrdee* |
| aubergine | melanzana | *maylahntzahnah* |
| August | agosto | *ahgosto* |
| automatic (car) | macchina con il cambio automatico | *mahkkeenah kon eel kahmbeeo ahootomahteeko* |
| automatic | automatico | *ahootomahteeko* |
| automatic shutter release | autoscatto | *ahootoskahtto* |
| autumn | autunno | *ahootoonno* |
| avalanche | valanga | *vahlahngah* |
| awake | sveglio | *svayllyo* |
| awning | tenda da sole | *tayndah dah solay* |

## B

| | | |
|---|---|---|
| baby | bambino/a | *bahmbeeno/ah* |
| baby food (jars of) | gli omogeneizzati | *lly omojaynayeedzahtee* |
| babysitter | la/il baby-sitter | *lah/eel baybeeseettayr* |
| back | schiena | *skeeaynah* |
| bacon | pancetta | *pahnchayttah* |
| bad | cattivo/male | *kahtteevo/mahlay* |
| bad/serious | grave | *grahvay* |
| bag | borsa | *borsah* |
| baker | panetteria | *pahnayttayreeah* |
| balcony (theatre) | galleria | *gahllayreeah* |
| balcony (to building) | il balcone | *eel bahlkonay* |
| ball | il pallone | *eel pahllonay* |
| ballet | balletto | *bahllaytto* |
| ballpoint pen | la biro | *lah beero* |
| banana | banana | *bahnahnah* |
| bandage | fascia | *fahsheeah* |
| bank (river) | riva | *reevah* |
| bank | banca | *bahnkah* |
| bar (café) | il bar | *eel bahr* |
| bar (drinks cabinet) | il bar | *eel bahr* |
| barbecue | il barbecue | *eel bahrbaykeeoo* |
| basketball (to play) | giocare a pallacanestro | *jokahray ah pahllahkahnaystro* |
| bath | bagno | *bahneeo* |
| bath towel | asciugamano da bagno | *ahshoogahmahno dah bahneeo* |
| bathing cap | cuffia da bagno | *cooffeeah dah bahneeo* |
| bathing cubicle | cabina | *kahbeenah* |
| bathing suit | il costume da bagno | *eel kostoomay dah bahneeo* |
| bathroom | bagno | *bahneeo* |
| battery (car) | batteria | *bahttayreeah* |
| battery | pila | *peellah* |
| beach | spiaggia | *speeahdjah* |
| beans | i fagioli | *ee fahjolee* |
| beautiful | bello | *bayllo* |
| beauty parlour | istituto di bellezza | *eesteetooto dee bayllaytzah* |
| bed | letto | *laytto* |
| bee | ape (f) | *ahpay* |
| beef | manzo | *mahnzo* |
| beer | birra | *beerrah* |
| beetroot | barbabietola | *bahrbahbeeaytolah* |
| begin (verb) | cominciare | *komeencheeahray* |
| beginner | il/la principiante | *eel/lah preencheepeeahntay* |
| behind | dietro | *deeaytro* |
| belt | cintura | *cheentoorah* |
| berth | cuccetta | *kootchayttah* |
| better | meglio | *mayllyo* |
| bicarbonate of soda | bicarbonato | *beekahrbonahto* |
| bicycle | bicicletta | *beecheeklayttah* |
| bicycle pump | pompa della bicicletta | *pompah dayllah beecheeklayttah* |

| | | |
|---|---|---|
| bicycle/motorcycle repairs | riparazioni motociclette e biciclette | *reepahrahtzeeonee motocheeklayttay ay beecheeklayttay* |
| bikini | il bikini | *eel beekeenee* |
| bill | conto | *konto* |
| billiards, to play | giocare a biliardo | *jokahray ah beellyahrdo* |
| birthday | compleanno | *komplayahnno* |
| biscuit | biscotto | *beeskotto* |
| bite (verb) | mordere | *mordayray* |
| bitter | amaro | *ahmahro* |
| black | nero | *nayro* |
| bland | insipido | *eenseepeedo* |
| blanket | coperta | *kopayrtah* |
| bleach (verb) | ossigenare | *osseejaynahray* |
| blister | vescica | *vaysheekah* |
| blond | biondo | *beeondo* |
| blood | il sangue | *eel sahngway* |
| blood pressure | la pressione (del sangue) | *lah praysseeonay (dayl sahngway)* |
| blouse | camicetta | *kahmeechayttah* |
| blow dry (verb) | asciugare con il fon | *ahshoogahray kon eel fon* |
| blue | azzurro | *ahdzoorro* |
| boat | barca | *bahrkah* |
| body | corpo | *korpo* |
| body milk | il latte per il corpo | *eel lahttay payr eel korpo* |
| bone | osso | *osso* |
| bonnet | cofano | *kofahno* |
| book | libro | *leebro* |
| book (verb) | prenotare | *praynotahray* |
| booked | prenotato | *praynotahto* |
| booking office | ufficio prenotazioni | *ooffeecheeo praynotahtzeeonee* |
| bookshop | libreria | *leebrayreeah* |
| boot (car) | il baule | *eel bahoolay* |
| border | frontiera | *fronteeayrah* |
| bored (be) | annoiarsi | *ahnnoeeahrsee* |
| boring | noioso | *noeeozo* |
| born | nato | *nahto* |
| borrow | prendere in prestito | *prayndayray een praysteeto* |
| botanical garden | orto botanico | *orto botahneeko* |
| both | tutti e due | *toottee ay dooay* |
| bottle-warmer | lo scaldabiberon | *lo skahldah beebayron* |
| bottle (baby) | il biberon | *eel beebayron* |
| bottle | bottiglia | *botteellyah* |
| box (theatre) | palco | *pahlko* |
| box | scatola | *skahtolah* |
| boy | ragazzo | *rahgahtzo* |
| bra | reggiseno | *raydjeesayno* |
| bracelet | braccialetto | *brahtchahlaytto* |
| braised | stufato | *stoofahto* |
| brake | freno | *frayno* |

| | | |
|---|---|---|
| brake fluid | liquido dei freni | *leekweedo dayee fraynee* |
| brake oil | olio dei freni | *oleeo dayee fraynee* |
| brass | ottone (m) | *ottonay* |
| bread | il pane | *eel pahnay* |
| break (one's...) | rompersi (la...) | *rompayrsee (lah...)* |
| breakdown recovery | soccorso stradale | *sokkorso strahdahlay* |
| breakfast | la (prima) colazione | *lah (preemah) kolahtzeeonay* |
| breast | petto | *paytto* |
| bridge | il ponte | *eel pontay* |
| bring (verb) | portare | *portahray* |
| brochure | opuscolo | *opooskolo* |
| broken | rotto | *rotto* |
| brother | fratello | *frahtayllo* |
| brown | marrone | *mahrronay* |
| bruise | livido | *leeveedo* |
| brush | spazzola | *spahtzolah* |
| Brussels sprouts | i cavoletti di Bruxelles | *ee kahvolayttee dee Brooxayls* |
| bubble bath | il bagno schiuma | *eel bahneeo skeeoomah* |
| bucket | secchio | *saykkeeo* |
| bug | insetto | *eensaytto* |
| building | edificio | *aydeefeecho* |
| buoy | boa | *boah* |
| burglary | furto (con scasso) | *foorto (kon skahsso)* |
| burn | bruciatura | *broochahtoorah* |
| burn (verb) | bruciare | *broochahray* |
| burnt | bruciato | *broochahto* |
| bus | autobus (m) | *ahootoboos* |
| bus station | la stazione degli autobus | *lah stahtzeeonay daylly ahootoboos* |
| bus stop | fermata dell'autobus | *fayrmahtah dayll-ahootoboos* |
| business trip | viaggio d'affari | *veeahdjo dahffahree* |
| busy | occupato | *okkoopahto* |
| butane camping gas | bombola a gas butano | *bombolah ah gahs bootahno* |
| butcher | macellaio | *mahchayllaheeo* |
| butter | burro | *boorro* |
| buttered roll | panino (con burro) | *pahneeno (kon boorro)* |
| button | il bottone | *eel bottonay* |
| buy (verb) | comprare | *komprahray* |
| by airmail | via aerea | *veeah ahayrayah* |

## C

| | | |
|---|---|---|
| cabbage | cavolo | *kahvolo* |
| cabin | capanna | *kahpahnnah* |
| cake | torta | *tortah* |
| cake (small) | pasticcino | *pahsteetcheeno* |
| cake shop | pasticcieria | *pahsteetcheeayreeah* |
| call (verb) | telefonare/chiamare | *taylayfonahray/ keeahmahray* |
| call (verb) | chiamare | *keeahmahray* |
| called, to be | chiamarsi | *keeahmahrsee* |

| | | |
|---|---|---|
| camera | macchina fotografica | *mahkkeenah fotograhfeekah* |
| camp (verb) | campeggiare | *kahmpedjahray* |
| camp shop | il mini-market | *eel meenee-mahrkayt* |
| camp site | campeggio | *kahmpaydjo* |
| camper | il camper | *eel kahmper* |
| camping guide | guida dei campeggi | *gweedah dayee kahmpedjee* |
| camping permit | permesso di campeggiare | *payrmaysso dee kahmpedjahray* |
| canal boat | battello | *bahttayllo* |
| cancel (verb) | annullare | *ahnnoollahray* |
| candle | candela | *kahndaylah* |
| canoe | canoa | *kahnoah* |
| canoe (verb) | andare in canoa | *ahndahray een kahnoah* |
| car | macchina | *mahkkeenah* |
| car documents | i documenti della macchina | *ee dokoomayntee dayllah mahkkeenah* |
| car seat | il sedile | *eel saydeellay* |
| car trouble | panne | *pahnnay* |
| carafe | caraffa | *kahrahffah* |
| caravan | la roulotte | *lah roolot* |
| cardigan | il cardigan | *eel cahrdeegahn* |
| careful | attenzione | *ahttayntzeeonay* |
| carriage (railway) | il vagone | *eel vahgonay* |
| carriageway | carreggiata | *kahrraydjhahtah* |
| carrot | carota | *kahrotah* |
| carton (cigarettes) | stecca (di sigarette) | *stekkah (dee seegahrayttay)* |
| cartridge | cassetta | *kahssayttah* |
| cash desk | cassa | *kahssah* |
| casino | casinò | *kahzeeno* |
| cassette | cassetta | *kahssayttah* |
| castle | castello | *kahstayllo* |
| cat | gatto | *gahtto* |
| catalogue | catalogo | *kahtahlogo* |
| cathedral | la cattedrale | *lah kahttaydrahlay* |
| cauliflower | il cavolfiore | *eel kahvolfeeoray* |
| cave | grotta | *grottah* |
| CD | il compact (disk) | *eel kompahkt (deesk)* |
| celebrate (verb) | far festa | *fahr faystah* |
| cellotape | nastro adesivo | *nahstro ahdayzeevo* |
| cemetery | cimitero | *cheemeetayro* |
| centimetre | centimetro | *chaynteemaytro* |
| central heating | riscaldamento centrale | *reeskahldahmaynto chayntrahlay* |
| centre | centro | *chayntro* |
| chain | catena | *kahtaynah* |
| chair | sedia | *saydyeeah* |
| chambermaid | cameriera | *kahmayreeayrah* |
| chamois (leather) | camoscio | *kahmosho* |
| champagne | lo champagne | *lo shahmpahn* |
| change | resto | *raysto* |
| change (verb) | cambiare | *kahmbeeahray* |

| | | |
|---|---|---|
| change the baby's nappy (verb) | cambiare il pannolino | *kahmbeeahray eel pahnnoleeno* |
| change the oil (verb) | cambiare l'olio | *kahmbeeahray loleeo* |
| chapel | cappella | *kahppayllah* |
| charter flight | volo charter | *volo chahrtayr* |
| chat up (verb) | fare la corte | *fahray lah kortay* |
| check (verb) | controllare | *kontrollahray* |
| check in (verb) | fare il check in | *fahray eel chaykeen* |
| cheers | cin cin | *cheen cheen* |
| cheese (tasty, mild) | formaggio (saporito, delicato) | *formahdjo (sahporeeto, dayleekahto)* |
| chef | capo | *kahpo* |
| cheque | assegno | *ahssayneeo* |
| cheque card | carta assegni | *kahrtah ahssaynyee* |
| cherries | le ciliege | *lay cheelleeayjay* |
| chess (to play) | (giocare a) scacchi | *(jokahray ah) skahkkee* |
| chewing gum | il chewing gum | *eel chayweeng goom* |
| chicken | pollo | *pollo* |
| chicory | cicoria | *cheekoreeah* |
| child | bambino | *bahmbeeno* |
| child's seat (bicycle) | seggiolino | *saydjeeoleeno* |
| chilled | fresco | *fraysko* |
| chin | mento | *maynto* |
| chips | le patate fritte | *lay pahtahtay freettay* |
| chocolate | cioccolata | *chokkolahtah* |
| chocolate (a) | cioccolatino | *chokkolahteeno* |
| choose (verb) | scegliere | *shayllyayray* |
| chop | braciola | *brahcholah* |
| christian name | il nome | *eel nomay* |
| church | chiesa | *keeayzah* |
| cigar | sigaro | *seegahro* |
| cigar shop | tabacchi (m) | *tahbahkkee* |
| cigarette | sigaretta | *seegahrayttah* |
| cigarette paper | le cartine | *lay kahrteenay* |
| cine camera | cinepresa | *cheenaypraysah* |
| circle | cerchio | *chayrkeeo* |
| circus | circo | *cheerko* |
| city hall | municipio | *mooneecheepeeo* |
| city map | pianta | *peeahntah* |
| classical concert | concerto di musica classica | *konchayrto dee moozeekah klahsseekah* |
| clean | pulito | *pooleeto* |
| clean (verb) | pulire | *pooleeray* |
| clear | chiaro | *keeahro* |
| clearance | svendita | *svayndeetah* |
| closed | chiuso | *keeoozo* |
| closed off (road) | chiuso al traffico | *keeoozo ahl trahffeeko* |
| clothes | i vestiti | *ee vaysteetee* |
| clothes hanger | ometto | *omaytto* |
| clothes peg | molletta da bucato | *mollayttah dah bookahto* |
| clothing | abbigliamento | *ahbbeellyahmaynto* |
| coach | il pullman | *eel poollmahn* |
| coat | soprabito/cappotto | *soprahbeeto/kahppotto* |
| cockroach | lo scarafaggio | *lo skahrahfahdjo* |

| | | |
|---|---|---|
| cocoa | cacao | *kahkaho* |
| cod | merluzzo | *mayrlootzo* |
| coffee | il caffè | *eel kahffay* |
| coffee filter | filtro del caffè | *feelltro dayl kahffay* |
| cognac | il cognac | *eel koneeahk* |
| cold (adj ) | freddo | *frayddo* |
| cold | il raffreddore | *eel rahffrayddoray* |
| cold cuts | gli affettati | *lly ahffettahtee* |
| colleague | il/la collega | *eel/lah kollaygah* |
| collision | lo scontro | *lo skontro* |
| cologne | eau de toilette (f) | *o day twahlayt* |
| colour | il colore | *eel koloray* |
| colour pencils | le matite colorate | *lay mahteetay kolorahtay* |
| colour TV | il televisore a colori | *eel taylayveezoray ah koloree* |
| colouring book | album (m) da colorare | *ahlboom dah kolorahray* |
| comb | il pettine | *eel paytteenay* |
| come | venire | *vayneeray* |
| come back (verb) | ritornare | *reetornahray* |
| compartment | lo scompartimento | *lo skompahrteemaynto* |
| complaint (med) | disturbo | *deestoorbo* |
| complaint | reclamo | *rayklahmo* |
| complaints book | libro reclami | *leebro rayklahmy* |
| completely | del tutto | *dayl tootto* |
| compliment | complimento | *kompleemaynto* |
| compulsory | obbligatorio | *obbleegahtoryeeo* |
| concert | concerto | *konchayrto* |
| concert hall | sala dei concerti | *sahlah day konchayrtee* |
| concussion | la commozione cerebrale | *lah kommotzeeonay chayraybrahlay* |
| condensed milk | il latte condensato | *eel lahttay kondaynsahto* |
| condom | preservativo | *praysayrvahteevo* |
| congratulate (verb) | congratulare | *kongrahtoolahray* |
| connection | collegamento | *kollaygahmaynto* |
| constipation | stitichezza | *steeteekaytzah* |
| consulate | consolato | *konsolahto* |
| consultation | la consultazione | *lah konsooltahtzeeonay* |
| contact lens | la lente a contatto | *lah layntay ah kontahtto* |
| contact lens solution | liquido per lenti a contatto | *leekweedo payr layntee ah kontahtto* |
| contagious | contagioso | *kontahdjozo* |
| contraceptive | anticoncezionale (m) | *ahnteekonchaytzee-nahlay* |
| cook (verb) | cucinare | *koocheenahray* |
| cook | cuoco/a | *kwoko/ah* |
| copper | il rame | *eel rahmay* |
| copy | copia | *kopeeah* |
| corkscrew | il cavatappi | *eel kahvahtahppee* |
| corn flour | fecola di mais | *faykolah dee  mahees* |
| corner | angolo | *ahngolo* |
| correct | giusto | *joosto* |
| correspond (verb) | corrispondere | *korreespondayray* |
| corridor | corridoio | *korreedoeeo* |
| costume | il costume | *eel kostoomay* |

| | | |
|---|---|---|
| cot | lettino per il bambino | *laytteeno payr eel bahmbeeno* |
| cotton | il cotone | *eel kotonay* |
| cotton wool | il cotone idrofilo | *eel kotonay eedrofeello* |
| cough | la tosse | *lah tossay* |
| cough mixture | lo sciroppo per la tosse | *lo sheeroppo payr lah tossay* |
| counter | banco | *bahnko* |
| country | campagna | *kahmpahneeah* |
| country code | prefisso | *prayfeesso* |
| countryside | il paese | *eel pahaysay* |
| courgette | zucchina | *dzookkeenah* |
| course | cura | *koorah* |
| cousin | cugino/a | *koogeeno/ah* |
| crab | granchio | *grahnkeeo* |
| cream | panna | *pahnnah* |
| cream/ointment (med ) | pomata | *pomahtah* |
| credit card | carta di credito | *kahrtah dee kraydeeto* |
| crisps | le patatine | *lay pahtahteenay* |
| croissant | il cornetto | *eel kornaytto* |
| cross-country run | pista da fondo | *peestah dah fondo* |
| cross-country skiing | fare dello sci di fondo | *fahray dayllo shee dee fondo* |
| cross-country skis | gli sci da fondo | *lly shee dah fondo* |
| cross (the road) (verb) | attraversare (la strada) | *ahttrahvayrsahray (lah strahdah)* |
| crossing (sea) | traversata | *trahvayrsahtah* |
| cry (verb) | piangere | *peeahnjayray* |
| cubic metre | metro cubo | *maytro koobo* |
| cucumber | cetriolo | *chaytreeolo* |
| cuddly toy | giocattolo di pelouche | *jokahttolo dee payloosh* |
| cuff links | i gemelli | *ee jemayllee* |
| culottes | la gonna pantaloni | *lah gonnah pahntahlonee* |
| cup | tazza | *tahtzah* |
| curly | riccio | *reetcheeo* |
| current | la corrente | *lah korrayntay* |
| cushion | cuscino | *koosheeno* |
| custard | crema | *kraymah* |
| customary | in uso | *een oozo* |
| customs | dogana | *dogahnah* |
| customs check | controllo doganale | *kontrollo dogahnahlay* |
| cut (verb) | tagliare | *tahllyahray* |
| cutlery | le posate | *lay pozahtay* |
| cycling | ciclismo | *cheekleesmo* |

## D

| | | |
|---|---|---|
| dairy produce | i latticini | *ee lahtteecheenee* |
| damaged | danneggiato | *dahnnaydjahto* |
| dance (verb) | ballare | *bahllahray* |
| dandruff | forfora | *forforah* |
| danger | pericolo | *payreekolo* |
| dangerous | pericoloso | *payreekoloso* |
| dark | scuro | *skooro* |
| daughter | figlia | *feellyah* |

| | | |
|---|---|---|
| dawn | alba | *ahlbah* |
| day | giorno | *jorno* |
| day before yesterday | l'altro ieri | *lahltro eeayree* |
| dead | morto | *morto* |
| dear/expensive | caro | *kahro* |
| decaffeinated | decaffeinato | *daykahffayeenahto* |
| December | dicembre (m) | *deechaymbray* |
| deck chair | la sdraio | *lah zdraheeo* |
| declare (verb) | dichiarare | *deekeeahrahray* |
| deep | profondo | *profondo* |
| deep sea diving | gli sport subacquei | *lly sport soobahkwayee* |
| deepfreeze | il surgelatore | *eel soorjaylahtoray* |
| degrees | i gradi | *ee grahdee* |
| delay | ritardo | *reetahrdo* |
| delicious | ottimo | *otteemo* |
| dentist | il/la dentista | *eel/lah daynteestah* |
| dentures | dentiera | *daynteeayrah* |
| deodorant | il deodorante | *eel dayodorahntay* |
| department | reparto | *raypahrto* |
| department store | grande magazzino | *grahnday mahgahdzeeno* |
| departure | partenza | *pahrtaynzah* |
| departure time | ora di partenza | *orah dee pahrtaynzah* |
| depilatory cream | crema depilatoria | *kraymah daypeellahtoreeah* |
| deposit (verb) | deposito | *daypozeeto* |
| deposit | caparra | *kahpahrrah* |
| dessert | il dolce | *eel dolchay* |
| destination | la destinazione | *lah desteenahtzeeonay* |
| develop | sviluppare | *sveellooppahray* |
| diabetic | diabetico | *deeahbeteeko* |
| dial (verb) | fare | *fahray* |
| diamond | il diamante | *eel deeahmahntay* |
| diarrhoea | diarrea | *deeahrrayah* |
| dictionary | dizionario | *deetzeeonahreeo* |
| diesel | gasolio | *gahzoleeo* |
| diesel oil | olio per motori diesel | *oleeo payr motoree deesayl* |
| diet | dieta | *deeaytah* |
| difficulty | difficoltà | *deeffeekoltah* |
| dine (verb) | cenare | *chaynahray* |
| dining room | sala da pranzo | *sahlah dah prahntzo* |
| dining/buffet car | carrozza ristorante | *kahrrotza/ reestorahntay* |
| dinner | cena | *chaynah* |
| dinner jacket | lo smoking | *lo smokeeng* |
| direction | la direzione | *lah deeraytzeeonay* |
| directly | direttamente | *deerayttahmayntay* |
| dirty | sporco | *sporko* |
| disabled | disabile | *deezahbeellay* |
| disco | discoteca | *deeskotaykah* |
| discount | lo sconto | *lo skonto* |
| dish | piatto | *peeahtto* |
| dish of the day | piatto del giorno | *peeahtto dayl jorno* |
| disinfectant | il disinfettante | *Il deeseenfettahntay* |

| | | |
|---|---|---|
| distance | distanza | *deestahntzah* |
| distilled water | acqua distillata | *ahkwah deesteellahtah* |
| disturb (verb) | disturbare | *deestoorbahray* |
| disturbance | disturbo | *deestoorbo* |
| dive (verb) | tuffarsi | *tooffahrsee* |
| diving | gli sport subacquei | *lly sport soobahkwayee* |
| diving board | trampolino | *trahmpoleeno* |
| diving gear | attrezzatura da sub | *ahttraytzahtoorah dah soob* |
| divorced | divorziato | *deevortzeeahto* |
| DIY-shop | negozio fai-da-te | *negotzeeo fahee-dah-tay* |
| dizzy (be) | avere il capogiro | *ahvayray eel kahpogeero* |
| do (verb) | fare | *fahray* |
| doctor | medico | *maydeeko* |
| dog | il cane | *eel kahnay* |
| doll | bambola | *bahmbolah* |
| domestic | domestico | *domaysteeko* |
| done (cooked) | cotto | *kotto* |
| door | porta | *portah* |
| double | doppio | *doppeeo* |
| down | giù | *joo* |
| draught | esserci corrente | *ayssayrchee korrayntay* |
| draughts (play) | giocare a dama | *jokahray ah dahmah* |
| dream (verb) | sognare | *soneeahray* |
| dress | vestito | *vaysteeto* |
| dressing gown | vestaglia | *vaystahllyah* |
| drink (verb) | bere | *bayray* |
| drinking chocolate | cacao | *kahkaho* |
| drinking water | acqua potabile | *ahkwah potahbeellay* |
| drive (verb) | guidare | *gweedahray* |
| driver | autista (m/f) | *ahooteestah* |
| driving licence | la patente (di guida) | *lah pahtayntay (dee gweedah)* |
| drought | siccità | *seetcheetah* |
| dry (verb) | asciugare | *ahshoogahray* |
| dry | secco | *saykko* |
| dry clean (verb) | lavare a secco | *lahvahray ah sekko* |
| dry cleaner's | lavanderia a secco | *lahvahndayreeah ah saykko* |
| dry shampoo | lo shampoo in polvere | *lo shahmpo een polvayray* |
| dummy | succhiotto | *sookkeeotto* |
| during | durante | *doorahntay* |
| during the day | di giorno | *dee jorno* |

## E

| | | |
|---|---|---|
| ear | orecchio | *oraykkeeo* |
| ear, nose and throat (ENT) specialist | otorinolaringoiatra | *otoreenolahreengoee-ahtrah* |
| earache | il mal d'orecchio | *eel mahl dorekkeeo* |
| eardrops | le gocce per le orecchie | *lay gotchay payr lay oraykkeeay* |
| early | presto | *praysto* |

| | | |
|---|---|---|
| earrings | gli orecchini | *lly oraykkeenee* |
| earth | terra | *tayrrah* |
| earthenware | ceramica | *chayrahmeekah* |
| east | est | *ayst* |
| easy | facile | *fahcheellay* |
| eat (verb) | mangiare | *mahnjahray* |
| eczema | eczema (m) | *aykzaymah* |
| eel | anguilla | *ahngweellah* |
| egg | uovo | *wovo* |
| elastic band | elastico | *aylahsteeko* |
| electric | elettrico | *aylayttreeko* |
| electricity | la corrente | *lah korrayntay* |
| embassy | ambasciata | *ahmbahshahtah* |
| emergency brake | freno d'emergenza | *frayno demayrjayntzah* |
| emergency exit | uscita di sicurezza | *oosheetah dee seekooraytzah* |
| emergency number | numero d'emergenza | *noomayro daymayrjayntzah* |
| emergency phone | telefono d'emergenza | *taylayfono dee aymayrjayntzah* |
| emergency triangle | triangolo d'emergenza | *treeahngolo daymayrjayntzah* |
| emery board | limetta per le unghie | *leemayttah payr lay oongeeay* |
| empty | vuoto | *vwoto* |
| engaged (busy) | occupato | *okkoopahto* |
| England | Inghilterra | *eengeelltayrrah* |
| English | inglese | *eenglaysay* |
| enjoy (verb) | godere | *godayray* |
| envelope | busta | *boostah* |
| error | errore (m) | *ayrroray* |
| escort | accompagnatrice (f) | *ahkkompahneeah-treechay* |
| evening (in the) | di sera | *dee sayrah* |
| evening wear | abito da sera | *ahbeeto dah sayrah* |
| event | avvenimento | *ahvvayneemaynto* |
| everything | tutto | *tootto* |
| everywhere | dappertutto | *dahppayrtootto* |
| examine (verb) | visitare | *veeseetahray* |
| excavation | gli scavi | *lly skahvee* |
| excellent | eccellente | *aytchayllayntay* |
| exchange (verb) | cambiare | *kahmbeeahray* |
| exchange office | ufficio cambio | *ooffeecho kahmbeeo* |
| exchange rate | tasso di cambio | *tahsso dee kahmbeeo* |
| excursion | escursione (f) | *ayskoorseeonay* |
| excuse me | mi scusi | *mee skoozee* |
| excuse/pardon me | scusi | *skoozee* |
| exhibition | mostra | *mostrah* |
| exit | uscita | *oosheetah* |
| expenses | le spese | *lay spaysay* |
| expensive | caro | *kahro* |
| explain (verb) | spiegare | *speeaygahray* |
| express | diretto | *deeraytto* |
| external | esterno | *aystayro* |
| eye | occhio | *okkeeo* |

| | | |
|---|---|---|
| eye drops | le gocce per gli occhi | *lay gotchay payrlly okkee* |
| eye shadow | ombretto | *ombraytto* |
| eye specialist | oculista (m/f) | *okooleestah* |
| eyeliner | eye-liner (m) | *aheellaheenayr* |

## F

| | | |
|---|---|---|
| face | faccia | *fahtchah* |
| factory | fabbrica | *fahbbreekah* |
| faith | la fede | *lah fayday* |
| fall (verb) | cadere | *kahdayray* |
| family | famiglia | *fahmeellyah* |
| famous | famoso | *fahmoso* |
| farm | fattoria | *fahttoreeah* |
| farmer | agricoltore | *ahgreekoltoray* |
| fashion | moda | *modah* |
| fast | presto | *praysto* |
| father | il padre | *eel pahdray* |
| fault | colpa | *kolpah* |
| fax (verb | spedire un fax | *spaydeeray oon fahx* |
| February | febbraio | *faybbraheeo* |
| feel (verb) | sentire | *saynteeray* |
| feel sick (verb) | avere la nausea | *ahvayray lah nahoozayah* |
| fence | cancello | *kahnchayllo* |
| ferry | traghetto | *trahgaytto* |
| fever | la febbre | *lah faybbray* |
| fill (verb) | otturare (un dente) | *ottoorahray (oon dayntay)* |
| fill out (verb) | compilare | *kompeellahray* |
| filling | otturazione (f) | *ottoorahtzeeonay* |
| film (photographic) | rullino | *roolleeno* |
| film | il film | *eel feellm* |
| filter | filtro | *feelltro* |
| find (verb) | trovare | *trovahray* |
| fine (delicate) | fine | *feenay* |
| fine | multa | *mooltah* |
| finger | dito | *deeto* |
| fire | fuoco | *fwoko* |
| fire (accident) | incendio | *eenchayndeeo* |
| fire brigade | i pompieri/i vigili del fuoco | *ee pompee-ayree/ee veejeellee dayl fwoko* |
| fire escape | scala di sicurezza | *skahlah dee seekooraytzah* |
| fire extinguisher | estintore (m) | *aysteentoray* |
| first | primo | *preemo* |
| first aid | pronto soccorso | *pronto sokkorso* |
| first class | prima classe | *preemah klahssay* |
| fish (verb) | pescare | *peskahray* |
| fish | il pesce | *eel payshay* |
| fishing rod | canna da pesca | *kahnnah dah payskah* |
| fitness centre | palestra | *pahlaystrah* |
| fitness training | il fitness | *eel feetness* |
| fitting room | camerino | *kahmayreeno* |
| fix (verb) | aggiustare | *ahdjoostahray* |
| flag | bandiera | *bahndeeayrah* |

| | | |
|---|---|---|
| flash | il flash | *eel flash* |
| flash bulb | lampada flash | *lahmpahdah flash* |
| flash cube | cubo flash | *koobo flahsh* |
| flat | appartamento | *ahppahrtahmaynto* |
| flea market | mercato delle pulci | *mayrkahto dayllay poolchee* |
| flight | volo | *volo* |
| flight number | numero del volo | *noomayro dayl volo* |
| flood | inondazione (f) | *eenondahtzeeonay* |
| floor | piano | *peeahno* |
| flour | farina | *fahreenah* |
| flu | influenza | *eenflooayntzah* |
| fly-over | viadotto | *veeahdotto* |
| fly (verb) | andare in aereo | *ahndahray een ahayrayo* |
| fly (insect) | mosca | *moskah* |
| fog | nebbia | *naybbeeah* |
| foggy (be) | esserci nebbia | *ayssayrchee naybbeeah* |
| folkloristic | folcloristico | *folkloreesteeko* |
| follow (verb) | seguire | *saygweeray* |
| food | cibo | *cheebo* |
| food poisoning | intossicazione (f) alimentare | *eentosseekahtzeeonay ahleemayntahray* |
| foodstuffs | gli alimentari | *lly ahleemayntahree* |
| foot | il piede | *eel peeayday* |
| for hire | a nolo | *ah nolo* |
| forbidden | vietato | *veeaytahto* |
| forehead | la fronte | *lah frontay* |
| foreign | straniero | *strahnyayro* |
| forget (verb) | dimenticare | *deemaynteekahray* |
| fork | forchetta | *forkayttah* |
| form | modulo | *modoolo* |
| fort | fortezza | *fortaytzah* |
| forward (verb) | spedire | *spaydeeray* |
| fountain | fontana | *fontahnah* |
| fragrant | aromatizzato | *ahromahteedzahto* |
| frame (for glasses) | montatura | *montahtoorah* |
| franc | franco | *frahnco* |
| free (of charge) | gratis | *grahtees* |
| free | libero | *leebayro* |
| free time | tempo libero | *taympo leebayro* |
| freeze (verb) | gelare | *jaylahray* |
| French | francese | *frahnchaysay* |
| French bread | filoncino | *feelloncheeno* |
| fresh | fresco | *fraysko* |
| Friday | il venerdì | *eel vaynayrdee* |
| fried | fritto | *freetto* |
| friend | amico/a | *ahmeeko/ah* |
| friendly | gentile | *jaynteellay* |
| frightened (be) | avere paura | *ahvayray pahoorah* |
| fringe | frangetta | *frahnjayttah* |
| fruit | frutta | *froottah* |
| fruit juice | succo di frutta | *sookko dee froottah* |
| frying pan | padella | *pahdayllah* |
| full | pieno | *peeayno* |
| fun | divertimento | *deevayrteemaynto* |

# G

| | | |
|---|---|---|
| gallery | galleria | *gahllayreeah* |
| game | gioco | *joko* |
| garage | il garage | *eel gahrahdj* |
| garbage bag | sacco per i rifiuti | *sahkko payr ee reefeeootee* |
| garden | giardino | *jahrdeeno* |
| gastroenteritis | la gastroenterite | *lah gahstroayntayreetay* |
| gauze | garza idrofila | *gahrdzah eedrofeellah* |
| gear | marcia | *mahrchah* |
| gel | il gel | *eel jayl* |
| German | tedesco | *taydaysko* |
| get off | scendere | *shayndayray* |
| gift | regalo | *raygahlo* |
| gilt | dorato | *dorahto* |
| ginger | lo zenzero | *lo dzayndzayro* |
| girl | ragazza | *rahgahtzah* |
| girlfriend | amica | *ahmeekah* |
| giro cheque | assegno postale | *ahssayneeo postahlay* |
| giro pass | carta assegni | *kahrtah ahssaynee* |
| glacier | ghiacciaio | *geeahtcheeaeeo* |
| glass (tumbler) | il bicchiere | *eel beekkeeayray* |
| glass (wine) | vetro | *vaytro* |
| glasses | gli occhiali | *lly okkeeahlee* |
| glove | guanto | *gwahnto* |
| glue | colla | *kollah* |
| gnat | zanzara | *dzahndzahrah* |
| go | andare | *ahndahray* |
| go back (verb) | ritornare | *reetornahray* |
| go for a walk (verb) | fare una passeggiata | *fahray oonah pahssaydjeahtah* |
| go out (verb) | uscire | *oosheeray* |
| goat's cheese | formaggio caprino | *formahdjo kahpreeno* |
| gold | oro | *oro* |
| golf (play) | giocare a golf | *jokahray ah golf* |
| golf course | campo da golf | *kahmpo dah golf* |
| gone | sparito | *spahreeto* |
| good afternoon | buongiorno | *bwonjorno* |
| good evening | buonasera | *bwonahsayrah* |
| good morning | buongiorno | *bwonjorno* |
| good night | buonanotte | *bwonahnottay* |
| goodbye | addio | *ahddeeo* |
| gram | grammo | *grahmmo* |
| grandchild | il/la nipote | *eel/lah neepotay* |
| grandfather | nonno | *nonno* |
| grandmother | nonna | *nonnah* |
| grape | uva | *oovah* |
| grape juice | succo d'uva | *sookko doovah* |
| grapefruit | pompelmo | *pompaylmo* |
| grave | tomba | *tombah* |
| grease | grasso | *grahsso* |
| green | verde | *vayrday* |
| green card | carta verde | *kahrtah vayrday* |
| greet (verb) | salutare | *sahlootahray* |
| grey | grigio | *greejo* |
| grill (verb) | grigliare | *greellyahray* |

| | | |
|---|---|---|
| grilled | alla griglia | *ahllah greellyah* |
| grocer | gli alimentari | *lly ahleemayntahree* |
| ground | terra | *tayrrah* |
| group | gruppo | *grooppo* |
| guest house | la pensione | *lah paynseeonay* |
| guide (book) | guida | *gweedah* |
| guide (person) | guida | *gweedah* |
| guided tour | visita guidata | *veeseetah gweedahtah* |
| gynaecologist | ginecologo | *jeenaykologo* |

## H

| | | |
|---|---|---|
| hair | i capelli | *ee cahpaylly* |
| hairbrush | spazzola | *spahtzolah* |
| hairdresser | il parrucchiere | *eel pahrrookkeeayray* |
| hairpins | le forcine | *lay forcheenay* |
| hairspray | lacca | *lahkkah* |
| half | metà | *maytah* |
| half full | pieno a metà | *peeayno ah maytah* |
| half/middle | mezzo | *maydzo* |
| ham (boiled) | prosciutto (cotto) | *proshootto (kotto)* |
| ham (raw) | prosciutto (crudo) | *proshootto (kroodo)* |
| hammer | martello | *mahrtayllo* |
| hand | la mano | *lah mahno* |
| hand brake | freno a mano | *frayno ah mahno* |
| hand-glider | deltaplano | *dayltahplahno* |
| handbag | borsa | *borsah* |
| handkerchief | fazzoletto | *fahtzolaytto* |
| handmade | fatto a mano | *fahtto ah mahno* |
| happy | felice | *fayleechay* |
| harbour | porto | *porto* |
| hard | duro | *dooro* |
| hat | cappello | *kahppayllo* |
| have a light (verb) | avere da accendere | *ahvayray dah ahtchayndayray* |
| hayfever | la febbre da fieno | *lah febbray dah feeayno* |
| hazelnut | nocciola | *notcholah* |
| head | testa | *taystah* |
| headache | il mal di testa | *eel mahl dee testah* |
| health | la salute | *lah sahlootay* |
| health food shop | erboristeria | *ayrboreestayreeah* |
| hear (verb) | sentire | *saynteeray* |
| hearing aid | apparecchio acustico | *ahppahraykkeeo ahkoosteeko* |
| heart | il cuore | *eel kworay* |
| heart patient | malato di cuore | *mahlahto dee kworay* |
| heat | il caldo | *eel kahldo* |
| heater | riscaldamento | *reeskahldahmaynto* |
| heavy | pesante | *payzahntay* |
| heel | calcagno | *kahlkahneeo* |
| heel (shoe) | tacco | *tahkko* |
| hello, goodbye | ciao | *chaho* |
| helmet | casco | *kahsko* |
| help (verb) | aiutare/dare una mano | *aeeootahray/dahray oonah mahno* |
| help | aiuto | *aheeooto* |

| | | |
|---|---|---|
| helping (of food) | la porzione | *lah portzeeonay* |
| herbal tea | infuso | *eenfooso* |
| herbs | le erbe aromatiche | *lay ayrbay ahromahteekay* |
| here | qui | *kwee* |
| herring | aringa | *ahreengah* |
| high | alto | *ahlto* |
| high tide | alta marea | *ahltah mahrayah* |
| highchair | il seggiolone | *eel saydjeeolonay* |
| hiking boots | gli scarponi | *lly skahrponee* |
| hip | anca | *ahnkah* |
| hire | prendere a nolo | *prayndayray ah nolo* |
| historic town centre | centro storico | *chayntro storeeko* |
| hitchhike (verb) | fare l'autostop | *fahray lahootostop* |
| hobby | hobby (m) | *obbee* |
| hold-up | colpo di mano | *kolpo dee mahno* |
| holiday (public) | giorno festivo | *jorno faysteevo* |
| holiday park | villaggio turistico | *veellahdjeeo tooreesteeko* |
| holidays | le vacanze | *lay vahkahntzay* |
| homesickness | nostalgia | *nostahljeeah* |
| honest | onesto | *onaysto* |
| honey | il miele | *eel meeayllay* |
| horizontal | orizzontale | *oreedzontahlay* |
| horrible | orribile | *orreebeellay* |
| horse | cavallo | *kahvahllo* |
| hospital | ospedale (m) | *ospaydahlay* |
| hospitality | ospitalità | *ospeetahleetah* |
| hot-water bottle | borsa dell'acqua calda | *borsah dayllahkwah kahldah* |
| hot, warm | caldo | *kahldo* |
| hotel | albergo | *ahlbayrgo* |
| hour | ora | *orah* |
| house | casa | *kahsah* |
| household items | i casalinghi | *ee kahsahleengee* |
| houses of parliament | palazzo del parlamento | *pahlahtzo dayl pahrlahmaynto* |
| housewife | casalinga | *kahsahleengah* |
| how far? | quanto è lontano? | *kwahnto ay lontahno?* |
| how long? | quanto tempo? | *kwahnto taympo?* |
| how much? | quanto? | *kwahnto?* |
| hundred grams | etto | *aytto* |
| hungry (be) | avere fame | *ahvayray fahmay* |
| hurricane | uragano | *oorahgahno* |
| hurry | fretta | *frayttah* |
| husband | marito | *mahreeto* |
| hut | cabina | *kahbeenah* |
| hyperventilation | iperventilazione (f) | *eepayrvaynteellah-tzeeonay* |

## I

| | | |
|---|---|---|
| ice (cubes) | ghiaccio | *gheeahtcheeo* |
| ice skate (verb) | pattinare | *pahtteenahray* |
| icecream | gelato | *jaylahto* |
| idea | idea | *eedayah* |
| identify (verb) | identificare | *eedaynteefeekahray* |
| identity card | carta d'identità | *kahrtah deedaynteetah* |

| | | |
|---|---|---|
| ignition key | la chiave d'accensione | *lah keeahvay dahtchaynseeonay* |
| ill | malato | *mahlahto* |
| illness | malattia | *mahlahtteeah* |
| imagine (verb) | immaginarsi | *eemmahjeennahrsee* |
| immediately | subito | *soobeeto* |
| import duty | tassa d'importazione | *tahssah deemportahtzeeonay* |
| impossible | impossibile | *eemposseebeellay* |
| in | in | *een* |
| in love with (be) | essere innamorato di | *essayray eennahmorahto dee* |
| included | incluso | *eenklooso* |
| indicate (verb) | indicare | *eendeekahray* |
| indicator | indicatore (m) di direzione | *eendeekahtoray dee deeraytzeeonay* |
| inexpensive | a buon mercato | *ah bwon mayrkahto* |
| infection (viral, bacterial) | infezione (f) (virale, batterica) | *eenfetzeeonay (veerahlay, bahttayreekah)* |
| inflammation | infiammazione (f) | *eenfeeahmmahtzeeo-nay* |
| information | informazione (f) | *eenformahtzeeonay* |
| information office | ufficio informazioni | *ooffeecheeo eenformahtzeeonee* |
| injection | iniezione (f) | *eenyeetzeeonay* |
| injured | ferito | *fayreeto* |
| inner ear | orecchio interno | *oraykkeeo eentayrno* |
| inner tube | camera d'aria | *kahmayrah dahreeah* |
| innocent | innocente | *eennochayntay* |
| insect | insetto | *eensaytto* |
| insect bite | puntura d'insetto | *poontoorah deensaytto* |
| insect repellant | insettifugo | *eensaytteefoogo* |
| inside | dentro | *dayntro* |
| insole | soletta | *solayttah* |
| insurance | assicurazione (f) | *ahsseekoorahtzeeonay* |
| intermission | intervallo | *eentayrvahllo* |
| international | internazionale | *eentayrnahtzeeonahlay* |
| interpreter | interprete (m/f) | *eentayrpraytay* |
| intersection, crossing | incrocio | *eenkrocheeo* |
| introduce (verb) | presentare | *praysayntahray* |
| invite (verb) | invitare | *eenveetahray* |
| iodine | (tintura di) iodio | *(teentoorah dee) eeodeeo* |
| Ireland | Irlanda | *Eerlahndah* |
| iron (metal) | ferro | *fayrro* |
| iron (verb) | stirare | *steerahray* |
| iron | ferro da stiro | *fayrro dah steero* |
| ironing board | tavolo da stiro | *tahvolo dah steero* |
| island | isola | *eezolah* |
| Italian | italiano | *eetahleeahno* |
| itch | prurito | *prooreeto* |

## J

| | | |
|---|---|---|
| jack | il cric | *eel kreek* |
| jacket | giacca | *jahkkah* |
| jam | marmellata | *mahrmayllahtah* |
| January | gennaio | *jaynnaheeo* |
| jar | barattolo | *bahrahttolo* |
| jaw | mascella | *mahshayllah* |
| jellyfish | medusa | *maydoosah* |
| jeweller | gioielleria | *joeeayllayreeah* |
| jewellery | i gioielli | *ee joyayllee* |
| jog (verb) | fare il footing | *fahray eel footeeng* |
| joke | lo scherzo | *lo skayrtzo* |
| juice | succo | *sookko* |
| July | luglio | *loolyo* |
| jumble sale | vendita di beneficenza | *vayndeetah dee baynayfeechayntzah* |
| jump leads | cavetto del caricabatteria | *kahvetto dayl kahreekahbahttayree-ah* |
| jumper | il maglione | *eel mahllyonay* |
| June | giugno | *jooneeo* |

## K

| | | |
|---|---|---|
| key | la chiave | *lah keeahvay* |
| kilo | chilo | *keello* |
| kilometre | chilometro | *keellomaytro* |
| kind | simpatico | *seempahteeko* |
| king | il re | *eel ray* |
| kiss (verb) | baciare | *bahcheeahray* |
| kiss | bacio | *bahcheeo* |
| kitchen | cucina | *koocheenah* |
| knee | ginocchio | *jeenokkeeo* |
| knee socks | i calzettoni | *ee kahltzettonee* |
| knife | coltello | *koltayllo* |
| knit | lavorare a maglia | *lahvorahray ah mahleeah* |
| know (verb) | sapere | *sahpayray* |

## L

| | | |
|---|---|---|
| lace | pizzo | *peetzo* |
| ladies toilet | gabinetto per signore | *gahbeenaytto payr seeneeoray* |
| lake | lago | *lahgo* |
| lamp | lampada | *lahmpahdah* |
| land (verb) | atterrare | *ahttayrrahray* |
| lane | corsia | *korseeah* |
| language | lingua | *leengwah* |
| lard | lardo | *lahrdo* |
| large | grande | *grahnday* |
| last | ultimo | *oolteemo* |
| last night | ieri notte | *eeayree nottay* |
| late | tardi | *tahrdee* |
| later | più tardi | *peeoo tahrdee* |
| laugh (verb) | ridere | *reedayray* |
| launderette | lavanderia | *lahvahndayreeah* |

| | | |
|---|---|---|
| law | diritto | *deereetto* |
| laxative | lassativo | *lahssahteevo* |
| leather | la pelle/cuoio | *lah payllay/kwoeeo* |
| leather goods | pelletteria | *payllayttayreeah* |
| leave (verb) | partire | *pahrteeray* |
| leek | porro | *porro* |
| left (on the) | a sinistra | *ah seeneestrah* |
| left | sinistra | *seeneestrah* |
| left luggage | deposito bagagli | *daypozeeto bahgahlly* |
| leg | gamba | *gahmbah* |
| lemon | il limone | *eel leemonay* |
| lend | prestare | *praystahray* |
| lens | obiettivo | *obeeaytteevo* |
| lentils | le lenticchie | *lay laynteekkyeeay* |
| less | meno | *mayno* |
| lesson | la lezione | *lah laytzeeonay* |
| letter | lettera | *layttayrah* |
| lettuce | lattuga | *lahttoogah* |
| level crossing | passaggio a livello | *pahssahdjeeo ah leevayllo* |
| library | biblioteca | *beebleeotaykah* |
| lie (verb) | mentire | *maynteeray* |
| life guard | bagnino | *bahneeno* |
| lift (hitchhike) | passaggio | *pahssahdjo* |
| lift (in building) | ascensore (m) | *ahshaynsoray* |
| lift (ski) | seggiovia | *saydjeeoveeah* |
| light (not dark) | chiaro | *keeahro* |
| light (not heavy) | leggero | *ledjayro* |
| lighter | accendino | *ahtchayndeeno* |
| lighthouse | faro | *fahro* |
| lightning | il fulmine | *eel foolmeenay* |
| like (verb) | piacere | *peeahchayray* |
| line | linea | *leenayah* |
| linen | lino | *leeno* |
| lipstick | rossetto | *rossaytto* |
| liquorice | liquerizia | *leekwayreetzeeah* |
| listen (verb) | ascoltare | *ahskoltahray* |
| literature | letteratura | *layttayrahtoorah* |
| litre | litro | *leetro* |
| little | poco | *poko* |
| live (verb) | abitare | *ahbeetahray* |
| live together (verb) | vivere insieme | *veevayray eenseeaymay* |
| lobster | aragosta | *ahrahgostah* |
| local | locale | *lokahlay* |
| lock | serratura | *sayrrahtoorah* |
| long | lungo | *loongo* |
| look (verb) | guardare | *gwahrdahray* |
| look for (verb) | cercare | *chayrkahray* |
| lorry | il camion | *eel kahmeeon* |
| lose (verb) | perdere | *payrdayray* |
| loss | perdita | *payrdeetah* |
| lost (be) | perdersi | *payrdayrsee* |
| lost | perso | *payrso* |
| lost item | oggetto smarrito | *odjaytto zmahrreeto* |

| | | |
|---|---|---|
| lost property office | ufficio oggetti smarriti | *ooffeecheeo odjayttee smahrreetee* |
| lotion | la lozione | *lah lotzeeonay* |
| loud | forte | *fortay* |
| love | amore (m) | *ahmoray* |
| love (verb) | amare | *ahmahray* |
| low | basso | *bahsso* |
| low tide | bassa marea | *bahssah mahrayah* |
| LPG | il gas liquido | *eel gahs leeqweedo* |
| luck | fortuna | *fortoonah* |
| luggage | i bagagli | *ee bahgahlly* |
| luggage locker | armadietto | *ahrmahdeeaytto* |
| lunch | pranzo | *prahntzo* |
| lungs | i polmoni | *ee polmonee* |

## M

| | | |
|---|---|---|
| macaroni | i maccheroni | *ee mahkkayronee* |
| madam | signora | *seeneeorah* |
| magazine | rivista | *reeveestah* |
| mail | posta | *postah* |
| main post office | posta centrale | *postah chayntrahlay* |
| main road | strada maestra | *strahdah mahaystrah* |
| make an appointment (verb) | fissare un appuntamento | *feessahray oon ahppoontahmaynto* |
| make love | fare l'amore | *fahray lahmoray* |
| makeshift | provvisorio | *provveezoreeo* |
| man | uomo | *womo* |
| manager | il direttore | *eel deerayttoray* |
| mandarin | mandarino | *mahndahreeno* |
| manicure | manicure | *mahneekooray* |
| map | pianta/mappa | *peeahntah/mahppah* |
| marble | marmo | *mahrmo* |
| March | marzo | *mahrtzo* |
| margarine | margarina | *mahrgahreenah* |
| marina | porto turistico | *porto tooreesteeko* |
| market | mercato | *mayrkahto* |
| marriage | matrimonio | *mahtreemoneeo* |
| married | sposato | *sposahto* |
| marry (verb) | sposarsi | *sposahrsee* |
| mass | messa | *mayssah* |
| massage | massaggio | *mahssahdjo* |
| mat | opaco | *opahko* |
| match | partita | *pahrteetah* |
| matches | i fiammiferi | *ee feeahmmeefayree* |
| May | maggio | *mahdjo* |
| maybe | forse | *forsay* |
| mayonnaise | la maionese | *lah maheeonaysay* |
| mayor | sindaco | *seendahko* |
| meal | pasto | *pahsto* |
| mean (verb) | significare | *seeneefeekkahray* |
| meat | la carne | *lah kahrnay* |
| medication | farmaco | *fahrmahko* |
| medicine | medicina | *maydeecheenah* |
| meet (verb) | conoscere | *konoshayray* |
| melon | il melone | *eel maylonay* |
| member (be a) | essere socio | *essayray socho* |

| | | |
|---|---|---|
| menstruate (verb) | avere le mestruazioni | *ahvayray lay maystrooahtzeeonee* |
| menstruation | la mestruazione | *lah maystrooahtzeeonee* |
| menu | il menù | *eel maynoo* |
| menu of the day | il menù del giorno | *eel maynoo dayl jorno* |
| message | messaggio | *mayssahdjo* |
| metal | metallo | *maytahllo* |
| meter (in cab) | tassametro | *tahssahmaytro* |
| metre | metro | *maytro* |
| migraine | emicrania | *aymeekrahneeah* |
| mild (tobacco) | leggero | *ledjeeayro* |
| milk | il latte | *eel lahttay* |
| millimetre | millimetro | *meelleemaytro* |
| mince | la carne tritata | *lah kahrnay treetahtah* |
| mineral water | acqua minerale | *ahkwah meenayrahlay* |
| minute | minuto | *meenooto* |
| mirror | lo specchio | *lo spekkeeo* |
| miss (verb) | mancare | *mahnkahray* |
| missing (be) | essere sparito | *essayray spahreeto* |
| missing (be) (verb) | mancare | *mahnkahray* |
| mistake | lo sbaglio | *lo sbahllyo* |
| mistaken (be) | sbagliarsi | *sbahllyahrsee* |
| misunderstanding | malinteso | *mahleentayzo* |
| modern art | arte moderna | *ahrtay modayrnah* |
| moment | attimo/momento | *ahtteemo/momaynto* |
| monastery | monastero | *monahstayro* |
| Monday | il lunedì | *eel loonaydee* |
| money | i soldi | *ee soldee* |
| month | il mese | *eel maysay* |
| moped | motorino | *motoreeno* |
| morning-after pill | pillola del giorno dopo | *peellolah dayl jorno dopo* |
| morning (in the) | la mattina | *lah mahtteenah* |
| mosque | moschea | *moskayah* |
| motel | il motel | *eel motayl* |
| mother | la madre | *lah mahdray* |
| motor cross | il motocross | *eel motocross* |
| motorbike | la moto(cicletta) | *lah moto(cheeklayttah)* |
| motorboat | motoscafo | *motoskahfo* |
| motorway | autostrada | *ahootostrahdah* |
| mountain | montagna | *montahneeah* |
| mountain hut | rifugio alpino | *reefoojo ahlpeeno* |
| mountaineering | alpinismo | *ahlpeeneesmo* |
| mouse | topo | *topo* |
| mouth | bocca | *bokkah* |
| much/many | molto/molti | *molto/moltee* |
| multi-storey car park | parcheggio a pagamento | *pahrkedjeeo ah pahgahmaynto* |
| muscle | muscolo | *mooskolo* |
| muscle spasms | i crampi muscolari | *ee krahmpee mooskolahree* |
| museum | museo | *moozayo* |
| mushrooms | i funghi | *ee foonghee* |
| music | musica | *moozeekah* |
| musical | il musical | *eel moozeekahl* |

| | | |
|---|---|---|
| mussels | le cozze | *lay kotzay* |
| mustard | la senape | *lah saynahpay* |

## N

| | | |
|---|---|---|
| nail (on hand) | unghia | *oongeeah* |
| nail | chiodo | *keeodo* |
| nail polish | lo smalto per le unghie | *lo smahlto payr lay oongheeay* |
| nail scissors | le forbicine per unghie | *lay forbeecheenay payr oongheeay* |
| naked | nudo | *noodo* |
| nappy | pannolino | *pahnnoleeno* |
| National Health Service | servizio sanitario | *sayrveetzeeo sahneetahreeo* |
| nationality | nazionalità | *nahtzeeonahleetah* |
| natural | naturale | *nahtoorahlay* |
| nature | natura | *nahtoorah* |
| naturism | naturismo | *nahtooreezmo* |
| near | presso | *praysso* |
| nearby | vicino | *veecheeno* |
| necessary | necessario | *nechayssahreeo* |
| neck | collo | *kollo* |
| nectarine | la pescanoce | *lah peskahnochay* |
| needle | ago | *ahgo* |
| negative | negativa | *naygahteevah* |
| neighbours | i vicini | *ee veecheenee* |
| nephew | il nipote | *eel neepotay* |
| never | mai | *mahee* |
| new | nuovo | *nwovo* |
| news | le notizie | *lay noteetzeeay* |
| news stand | edicola | *aydeekolah* |
| newspaper | il giornale | *eel jornahlay* |
| next | prossimo | *prosseemo* |
| next to | accanto a | *ahkkahnto ah* |
| nice | piacevole/bello/ buono | *peeahchayvolay/ bayllo/bwono* |
| niece | la nipote | *lah neepotay* |
| night | la notte | *lah nottay* |
| night duty | servizio notturno | *sayrveetzeeo nottoorno* |
| night-club | il locale notturno | *eel lokahlay nottoorno* |
| nightclub | il night | *eel naheet* |
| nightlife | vita notturna | *veetah nottoornah* |
| no-one | nessuno | *nessoono* |
| no | no | *no* |
| no overtaking | divieto di sorpasso | *deeveeayto dee sorpahsso* |
| noise | il rumore | *eel roomoray* |
| nonsense | le sciocchezze | *lay shokkaytzay* |
| nonstop | senza scalo | *saynzah skahlo* |
| normal | normale | *normahlay* |
| north | nord | *nord* |
| nose | naso | *nahzo* |
| nose drops | le gocce per il naso | *lay gotchay payr eel nahzo* |
| notepaper | carta da lettere | *kahrtah dah layttayray* |
| nothing | niente | *neeayntay* |

| | | |
|---|---|---|
| November | novembre (m) | *novaymbray* |
| nowhere | da nessuna parte | *dah nessoonah pahrtay* |
| nudist beach | spiaggia per nudisti | *speeahdjah payr noodeestee* |
| number | numero | *noomayro* |
| number plate | targa | *tahrgah* |
| nurse | infermiera | *eenfayrmeeayrah* |
| nutmeg | la noce moscata | *lah nochay moskahtah* |
| nuts | le noci | *lay nochee* |

## O

| | | |
|---|---|---|
| October | ottobre (m) | *ottobray* |
| odometer | il contachilometri | *eel kontahkeellomaytree* |
| off-licence | enoteca | *aynotaykah* |
| off (of food) | andato a male | *ahndahto ah mahlay* |
| offer (verb) | offrire | *offreeray* |
| office | ufficio | *ooffeecheeo* |
| oil (vegetable) | olio di semi | *oleeo dee saymee* |
| oil | olio | *oleeo* |
| oil level | livello dell'olio | *leevayllo daylloleeo* |
| ointment | pomata | *pomahtah* |
| ointment for burns | pomata contro le ustioni | *pomahtah kontro lay oosteeonee* |
| okay | d'accordo | *dahkkordo* |
| old | vecchio | *vaykkeeo* |
| olive oil | olio d'oliva | *oleeo doleevah* |
| olives | le olive | *lay oleevay* |
| omelette | frittata/omelette (f) | *freettahtah/omaylayt* |
| on | su/sopra | *soo/soprah* |
| on board | a bordo | *ah bordo* |
| oncoming car | veicolo che viene in senso contrario | *vayeekolo kay veeaynay een saynso kontrahryeeo* |
| one-way traffic | senso unico | *saynso ooneeko* |
| onion | cipolla | *cheepollah* |
| open | aperto | *ahpayrto* |
| open (verb) | aprire | *ahpreeray* |
| open air (in the) | all'aperto | *ahllahpayrto* |
| opera | opera | *opayrah* |
| operate (verb) | operare | *opayrahray* |
| operator (telephone) | il/la centralinista | *eel/lah chayntrahleeneestah* |
| operetta | operetta | *opayrayttah* |
| opposite | di fronte a | *dee frontay ah* |
| optician | ottico | *otteeko* |
| orange | arancia | *ahrahnchah* |
| orange (adj) | arancione | *ahrahncheeonay* |
| orange juice | spremuta d'arancia | *spraymootah dahrahnchah* |
| order | ordinazione (f) | *ordeenahtzeeonay* |
| order (verb) | ordinare | *ordeenahray* |
| other | altro | *ahltro* |
| other side | lato opposto | *lahto opposto* |
| outing | gita | *jeetah* |
| outside | fuori | *foohoree* |

| | | |
|---|---|---|
| overtake (verb) | sorpassare | *sorpahssahray* |
| oysters | le ostriche | *lay ostreekay* |

## P

| | | |
|---|---|---|
| packed lunch | la colazione al sacco | *lah kolahtzeeonay ahl sahkko* |
| pain | il dolore/il male | *eel doloray/eel mahlay* |
| painkiller | analgesico | *ahnahljayzeeko* |
| paint | la vernice | *lah vayrneechay* |
| painting (art) | pittura | *peettoorah* |
| painting (object) | quadro | *kwahdro* |
| palace | palazzo | *pahlahtzo* |
| pan | padella/pentola | *pahdayllah/payntolah* |
| pancake | la crèpe | *lah krayp* |
| pants (ladies') | lo slip | *lo sleep* |
| pants, briefs | le mutande | *lay mootahnday* |
| panty liner | il salvaslip | *eel sahlvahsleep* |
| paper | carta | *kahrtah* |
| paraffin oil | olio di paraffina | *oleeo dee pahrahffeenah* |
| parasol | ombrellone (m) | *ombrayllonay* |
| parcel | pacchetto | *pahkkaytto* |
| parents | i genitori | *ee jayneetoree* |
| park | parco | *pahrko* |
| park (verb) | parcheggiare | *pahrkaydjeeahray* |
| parking space | parcheggio | *pahrkaydjeeo* |
| parsley | prezzemolo | *praytzaymolo* |
| part (spare) | pezzo di ricambio | *paytzo dee reekahmbeeo* |
| partner | il/la partner | *eel/lah pahrtner* |
| party | festa | *faystah* |
| passable | transitabile | *trahnseetahbeellay* |
| passenger | passeggero | *pahssaydjayro* |
| passport | passaporto | *pahssahporto* |
| passport photo | la foto tessera | *lah foto tessayrah* |
| patient | il/la paziente | *eel/lah pahtzeeentay* |
| pavement | il marciapiede | *eel mahrcheeahpeeayday* |
| pay (verb) | pagare | *pahgahray* |
| peach | pesca | *payskah* |
| peanuts | le noccioline | *lay notcheeoleenay* |
| pear | pera | *payrah* |
| peas | i piselli | *ee peezayllee* |
| pedal | il pedale | *eel pedahlay* |
| pedestrian crossing | attraversamento pedonale | *ahttrahvayrsahmaynto paydonahlay* |
| pedicure | il/la pedicure | *eel/lah paydeekooray* |
| pen | penna | *paynnah* |
| pencil | matita | *mahteetah* |
| penis | il pene | *eel paynay* |
| pepper (red, green) | il peperone (rosso, verde) | *eel paypayronay (rosso, vayrday)* |
| pepper | il pepe | *eel paypay* |
| performance | lo spettacolo/la rappresentazione | *lo spayttahkolo/lah rahppraysayntahtzeeo-nay* |

| | | |
|---|---|---|
| perfume | profumo | *profoomo* |
| perm (verb) | fare la permanente | *fahray lah payrmahnayntay* |
| perm | la permanente | *lah payrmahnayntay* |
| permit | licenza | *leechaynzah* |
| person | persona | *payrsonah* |
| personal | personale | *payrsonahlay* |
| petrol | benzina | *bayndzeenah* |
| petrol station | il distributore di benzina | *eel deestreebootoray dee bayndzeenah* |
| pets | gli animali domestici | *lly ahneemahlee domaysteechee* |
| pharmacy | farmacia | *fahrmahcheeah* |
| phone (verb) | telefonare | *taylayfonahray* |
| phone (tele-) | telefono | *taylayfono* |
| phone box | telefono pubblico | *taylayfono poobbleeko* |
| phone directory | elenco telefonico | *aylaynko taylayfoneeko* |
| phone number | numero di telefono | *noomayro dee taylayfono* |
| photocopier | la copiatrice | *lah copeeahtreechay* |
| photocopy (verb) | fotocopiare | *fotokopeeahray* |
| photocopy | fotocopia | *fotokopeeah* |
| photograph | la foto | *lah foto* |
| photograph (verb) | fotografare | *fotograhfahray* |
| pick up (verb) | andare/venire a prendere | *ahndahray/vayneeray ah prayndayray* |
| pickled | sott'aceto | *sottahchayto* |
| picnic | il picnic | *eel peekneek* |
| piece of clothing | capo di vestiario | *kahpo dee vaysteeahreeo* |
| pier | molo | *molo* |
| pigeon | il piccione | *eel peetcheeonay* |
| pill (contraceptive) | pillola (anticoncezionale) | *peellolah (ahnteekonchaytzeeo-nahlay)* |
| pillow | il guanciale | *eel gwahncheeahlay* |
| pillowcase | federa | *faydayrah* |
| pin | lo spillo | *lo speello* |
| pineapple | ananas (m) | *ahnahnahs* |
| pink | rosa | *rozah* |
| pipe | pipa | *peepah* |
| pipe tobacco | tabacco da pipa | *tahbahkko dah peepah* |
| pity | peccato | *pekkahto* |
| place of interest | monumento | *monoomaynto* |
| plan, map | la piantina | *lah peeahnteenah* |
| plant | pianta | *peeahntah* |
| plasters | i cerotti | *ee chayrottee* |
| plastic | plastica | *plahsteekah* |
| plastic bag | busta di plastica | *boostah dee plahsteekah* |
| plate | piatto | *peeahtto* |
| platform | binario | *beenahreeo* |
| play (a) | opera teatrale | *opayrah tayhahtrahlay* |
| play (verb) | giocare | *jokahray* |
| playground | parco giochi | *pahrko jokee* |
| playing cards | le carte da gioco | *lay kahrtay dah joko* |

| | | |
|---|---|---|
| pleasant | piacevole | *peeahchayvolay* |
| please | per favore | *payr fahvoray* |
| please (verb) | piacere | *peeahchayray* |
| pleasure | il piacere | *eel peeahchayray* |
| plum | prugna | *prooneeah* |
| pocketknife | temperino | *taympayreeno* |
| point (verb) | indicare | *eendeekahray* |
| poison | veleno | *vaylayno* |
| police | polizia | *poleetzeeah* |
| police station | questura | *kwaystoorah* |
| policeman | il vigile | *eel veejeellay* |
| pond | lo stagno | *lo stahneeo* |
| pony | il pony | *eel ponee* |
| pop concert | concerto pop | *konchayrto pop* |
| population | la popolazione | *lah popolahtzeeonay* |
| pork | la carne di maiale | *lah kahrnay dee maheeahlay* |
| port | (vino di) porto | *(veeno dee) porto* |
| porter (hotel) | portinaio | *porteeonaheeo* |
| porter (railway) | facchino | *fahkkeeno* |
| post code | il codice postale | *eel kodeechay postahlay* |
| post office | ufficio postale | *ooffeecheeo postahlay* |
| postage | affrancatura | *ahffrahnkahtoorah* |
| postbox | buca delle lettere | *bookah dayllay layttayray* |
| postcard | cartolina | *kahrtoleenah* |
| postman | postino | *posteeno* |
| potato | patata | *pahtahtah* |
| poultry | il pollame | *eel pollahmay* |
| powdered milk | il latte in polvere | *eel lahttay een polvayray* |
| power point | presa elettrica | *prayzah aylayttreekah* |
| power walking | podismo | *podeezmo* |
| pram | carrozzina | *kahrrotzeenah* |
| prawns | i gamberetti | *ee gahmbayrayttee* |
| prefer (verb) | preferire | *prefayreeray* |
| preference | preferenza | *prefayrayntzah* |
| pregnant | incinta | *eencheentah* |
| present (gift) | regalo | *regahlo* |
| present (in time) | presente | *prayzayntay* |
| press (verb) | pigiare | *peejahray* |
| pressure | la pressione | *lah praysseeonay* |
| price | prezzo | *praytzo* |
| price list | listino prezzi | *leesteeno praytzee* |
| print (verb) | stampare | *stahmpahray* |
| print | copia | *kopeeah* |
| probably | probabilmente | *probahbeellmayntay* |
| problem | il problema | *eel problaymah* |
| profession | la professione | *lah professeeonay* |
| programme | il programma | *eel prograhmmah* |
| pronounce (verb) | pronunciare | *pronoonchahray* |
| propane camping gas | bombola a gas propano | *bombolah ah gahs propahno* |
| prune | prugna secca | *prooneeah saykkah* |
| pudding | budino | *boodeeno* |

| | | |
|---|---|---|
| pull a muscle (verb) | avere uno strappo muscolare | *ahvayray oono strahppo mooskolahray* |
| pull out (a tooth) (verb) | estrarre (un dente) | *estrahrray (oon dayntay)* |
| pure | puro | *pooro* |
| purple | viola | *veeolah* |
| purse | il portamonete/ borsellino | *eel portahmonaytay/ borsaylleeno* |
| push (verb) | spingere | *speenjayray* |
| puzzle | il puzzle | *eel poodzlay* |
| pyjamas | il pigiama | *eel peejahmah* |

## Q

| | | |
|---|---|---|
| quarter | quarto | *kwahrto* |
| quarter of an hour | quarto d'ora | *kwahrto dorah* |
| queen | regina | *rayjeenah* |
| question | domanda | *domahndah* |
| quick | presto | *praysto* |
| quiet | tranquillo | *trahnkweello* |

## R

| | | |
|---|---|---|
| radio | la radio | *lah rahdeeo* |
| railways | le ferrovie | *lay fayrroveeay* |
| rain (verb) | piovere | *peeovayray* |
| rain | pioggia | *peeodjah* |
| raincoat | impermeabile (m) | *eempayrmayahbeellay* |
| raisin | uva secca | *oovah saykkah* |
| rape | lo stupro | *lo stoopro* |
| rapids | rapida | *rahpeedah* |
| raspberries | i lamponi | *ee lahmponee* |
| raw | crudo | *kroodo* |
| raw vegetables | le verdure crude | *lay vayrdooray krooday* |
| razor blades | le lamette | *lay lahmayttay* |
| read | leggere | *ledjayray* |
| ready | pronto | *pronto* |
| receipt (till) | lo scontrino | *lo skontreeno* |
| receipt | ricevuta | *reechayvootah* |
| recipe | ricetta | *reechayttah* |
| reclining chair | sedia a sdraio | *saydeeah ah sdraheeo* |
| recommend (verb) | consigliare | *konseellyahray* |
| rectangle | rettangolo | *rayttahngolahray* |
| red | rosso | *rosso* |
| red wine | vino rosso | *veeno rosso* |
| reduction | lo sconto | *lo skonto* |
| refrigerator | frigorifero | *freegoreefayro* |
| regards | (tanti) saluti | *(tahntee) sahlootee* |
| region | la regione | *lah rayjonay* |
| registered | raccomandato | *rahkkomahndahto* |
| registration (car) | libretto di circolazione | *leebraytto dee cheerkolahtzeeonay* |
| relatives | i parenti | *ee pahrayntee* |
| reliable | affidabile | *ahffeedahbeellay* |
| religion | la religione | *lah rayleejonay* |
| rent (verb) | affittare | *ahffeettahray* |
| rent out (verb) | affittare | *ahffeettahray* |

| | | |
|---|---|---|
| repair (verb) | aggiustare | *ahdjoostahray* |
| repairs | le riparazioni | *lay reepahrahtzeeonee* |
| repeat (verb) | ripetere | *reepaytayray* |
| report | il verbale | *eel vayrbahlay* |
| responsible | responsabile | *raysponsahbeellay* |
| rest (verb) | riposare | *reepozahray* |
| restaurant | il ristorante | *eel reestorahntay* |
| retired | pensionato | *paynseeonahto* |
| return (ticket) | andata e ritorno (f) | *ahndahtah ay reetorno* |
| reverse (vehicle) (verb) | fare marcia indietro | *fahray mahrchah eendeeaytro* |
| rheumatism | reumatismo | *rayoomahteezmo* |
| rice | riso | *reezo* |
| riding (horseback) | andare a cavallo | *ahndahray ah kahvahllo* |
| riding school | maneggio | *mahnaydjeeo* |
| right | destra | *daystrah* |
| right (on the) | a destra | *ah daystrah* |
| ripe | maturo | *mahtooro* |
| risk | rischio | *reeskeeo* |
| river | il fiume | *eel feeoomay* |
| road | strada | *strahdah* |
| roasted | arrostito | *ahrrosteeto* |
| rock | roccia | *rotchah* |
| roll (bread) | panino | *pahneeno* |
| rolling tobacco | tabacco per sigarette | *tahbahkko payr seegahrayttay* |
| roof rack | il portapacchi | *eel portahpahkkee* |
| room | camera | *kahmayrah* |
| room number | numero della camera | *noomayro dayllah kahmayrah* |
| room service | servizio in camera | *sayrveetzeeo een kahmayrah* |
| rope | corda | *kordah* |
| rosé | rosato | *rozahto* |
| roundabout | rotatoria | *rotahtoreeah* |
| route | itinerario | *eeteenayrahreeo* |
| rowing boat | barca a remi | *bahrkah ah raymee* |
| rubber | gomma | *gommah* |
| rubbish (silly things) | le sciocchezze | *lay shokkaytzay* |
| rucksack | lo zaino | *lo dzaheeno* |
| rude | scortese | *skortayzay* |
| ruins | le rovine | *lay roveenay* |
| run into (verb) | incontrare | *eenkontrahray* |

## S

| | | |
|---|---|---|
| sad | triste | *treestay* |
| safari | il safari | *eel sahfahree* |
| safe (adj) | sicuro | *seekooro* |
| safe | cassetta di sicurezza | *kahssayttah dee seekooraytzah* |
| safety pin | spilla di sicurezza | *speellah dee seekooraytzah* |
| sail (verb) | fare della vela | *fahray dayllah vaylah* |
| sailing boat | barca a vela | *bahrkah ah vaylah* |
| salad | insalata | *eensahlahtah* |
| salami | il salame | *eel sahlahmay* |
| sale | i saldi | *ee sahldee* |

| | | |
|---|---|---|
| salt | il sale | *eel sahlay* |
| same | lo stesso | *lo staysso* |
| sandy beach | spiaggia di sabbia | *speeahdjah dee sahbbeeah* |
| sanitary pads | gli assorbenti | *lly ahssorbayntee* |
| sardines | le sardine | *lay sahrdeenay* |
| satisfied | contento | *kontaynto* |
| Saturday | sabato | *sahbahto* |
| sauce | sugo | *soogo* |
| sausage | salsiccia | *sahlseetchah* |
| savoury | saporito | *sahporeeto* |
| say (verb) | dire | *deeray* |
| scarf | sciarpa | *shahrpah* |
| scenic walk | itinerario turistico | *eeteenayrahreeo tooreesteeko* |
| school | scuola | *skwolah* |
| scissors | le forbici | *lay forbeechee* |
| scooter | scooter | *skootayr* |
| scorpion | lo scorpione | *lo skorpeeonay* |
| Scotland | Scozia | *Scotzeeah* |
| scrambled eggs | le uova strapazzate | *lay wovah strahpahtzahtay* |
| screw | la vite | *lah veetay* |
| screwdriver | il cacciavite | *eel kahtchahveetay* |
| sculpture | scultura | *skooltoorah* |
| sea | il mare | *eel mahray* |
| seasick (be) | avere il mal di mare | *ahvayray eel mahldeemahray* |
| seat | posto (a sedere) | *posto (ah saydayray)* |
| second-hand | usato | *oozahto* |
| second | secondo | *saykondo* |
| secretion (med) | la secrezione | *lah saykraytzeeonay* |
| sedative | il tranquillante | *eel trahnkweellahntay* |
| see (verb) | vedere | *vedayray* |
| semi-skimmed | parzialmente scremato | *pahrtzeeahlmayntay skraymahto* |
| send (verb) | spedire | *spaydeeray* |
| sentence | la frase | *lah frahzay* |
| September | settembre (m) | *sayttaymbray* |
| service (church) | la funzione religiosa | *lah foontzeeonay rayleejozah* |
| service | servizio | *sayrveetzeeo* |
| serviette | tovagliolo | *tovahllyolo* |
| set (of hair) (verb) | mettere in piega | *mayttayray een peeaygah* |
| sewing thread | filo da cucire | *feello dah koocheeray* |
| shade | ombra | *ombrah* |
| shallow | poco profondo | *poko profondo* |
| shampoo | lo shampoo | *lo shahmpo* |
| shark | lo squalo | *lo skwahlo* |
| shave (verb) | farsi la barba | *fahrsee lah bahrbah* |
| shaver | rasoio | *rahzoyeeo* |
| shaving brush | pennello da barba | *paynnayllo dah bahrbah* |
| shaving cream | crema da barba | *kraymah dah bahrbah* |
| shaving soap | il sapone da barba | *eel sahponay dah bahrbah* |

| | | |
|---|---|---|
| sheet | lenzuolo | *laynzwolo* |
| sherry | Sherry | *Shayrree* |
| shirt | camicia | *kahmeechah* |
| shoe | scarpa | *skahrpah* |
| shoe polish | lucido da scarpe | *loocheedo dah skahrpay* |
| shoe shop | calzature | *kahltzahtooray* |
| shoelace | laccio | *lahtcheeo* |
| shoemaker | calzolaio | *kahltzolaheeo* |
| shop | negozio | *negotzeeo* |
| shop (verb) | fare la spesa | *fahray lah spayzah* |
| shop assistant | commessa/o | *kommayssah/o* |
| shop window | vetrina | *vaytreenah* |
| shopping centre | centro commerciale | *chayntro kommayrchahlay* |
| short | corto/breve | *korto/brayvay* |
| short circuit | cortocircuito | *kortocheerkweeto* |
| shoulder | spalla | *spahllah* |
| show | lo spettacolo | *lo spayttahkolo* |
| shower | doccia | *dotcheeah* |
| shutter | otturatore (m) | *ottoorahtoray* |
| side | lato | *lahto* |
| sieve | setaccio | *saytahtcho* |
| sign | cartello | *kahrtayllo* |
| sign (verb) | firmare | *feermahray* |
| silence | silenzio | *seellayntzeeo* |
| silver | argento | *ahrjaynto* |
| silver-plated | placcato in argento | *plahkkahto een ahrjaynto* |
| simple | semplice | *saympleechay* |
| single (ticket) | andata | *ahndahtah* |
| single (unmarried) | singolo | *seengolo* |
| single | singolo | *seengolo* |
| sir | il signore | *eel seeneeoray* |
| sister | sorella | *sorayllah* |
| sit (verb) | sedere | *saydayray* |
| size | misura/ taglia | *meezoorah/ tahllyah* |
| ski (verb) | sciare | *sheeahray* |
| ski boots | gli scarponi da sci | *lly skahrponee dah shee* |
| ski goggles | gli occhiali da sci | *lly okkeeahlee dah shee* |
| ski instructor | maestro di sci | *mahaystro dee shee* |
| ski lessons/class | la lezione di sci | *lah laytzeeonay dee shee* |
| ski lift | lo ski-lift | *lo skee-leeft* |
| ski pants | i pantaloni da sci | *ee pahntahlony dah shee* |
| ski pass | lo ski pass | *lo skee pahss* |
| ski slope | pista da sci | *peestah dah shee* |
| ski stick | racchetta | *rahkkayttah* |
| ski suit | completo da sci | *complayto dah shee* |
| ski wax | sciolina | *sheeoleenah* |
| skin | la pelle | *lah payllay* |
| skirt | gonna | *gonnah* |
| skis | paio di sci | *paheeo dee shee* |
| sleep (verb) | dormire | *dormeeray* |

| | | |
|---|---|---|
| sleeping car | la carrozza letto | *lah kahrrotzah laytto* |
| sleeping pills | i sonniferi | *ee sonneefayree* |
| slide | diapositiva | *deeahpozeeteevah* |
| slip | la sottoveste | *lah sottovaystay* |
| slip road | corsia di accelerazione | *korseeah dee ahtchaylayrahtzeeonay* |
| slow | lento | *laynto* |
| slow train | il locale | *eel lokahlay* |
| small | piccolo | *peekkolo* |
| small change | moneta | *monaytah* |
| smell (verb) | puzzare | *pootzahray* |
| smoke | fumo | *foomo* |
| smoke (verb) | fumare | *foomahray* |
| smoked | affumicato | *ahffoomeekahto* |
| smoking compartment | scompartimento per fumatori | *skompahrteemaynto payr foomahtoree* |
| snake | la serpe | *lah sayrpay* |
| snorkel | il boccaglio | *eel bokkahllyo* |
| snow (verb) | nevicare | *nayveekahray* |
| snow | la neve | *lah nayvay* |
| snow chains | le catene da neve | *lay kahtaynay dah nayvay* |
| soap | il sapone | *eel sahponay* |
| soap powder | il sapone in polvere | *eel sahponay een polvayray* |
| soccer | calcio | *kahlcho* |
| soccer match | partita di calcio | *pahrteetah dee kahlcho* |
| socket | presa di corrente | *prayzah dee korrayntay* |
| socks | i calzini | *ee kahltzeenee* |
| soft drink | bibita/ bevanda | *beebeetah/ bevahdah* |
| sole (fish) | sogliola | *sollyolah* |
| sole (shoe) | suola | *swolah* |
| solicitor | avvocato | *ahvvokahto* |
| someone | qualcuno | *kwahlkoono* |
| sometimes | talvolta | *tahlvoltah* |
| somewhere | da qualche parte | *dah kwahlkay pahrtay* |
| son | figlio | *feellyo* |
| soon | presto | *praysto* |
| sorbet | sorbetto | *sorbaytto* |
| sore | ulcera | *oolchayrah* |
| sore throat | il mal di gola | *eel mahl dee golah* |
| sorry | scusami/mi scusi | *skoozahmee/mee skoozee* |
| sort | tipo | *teepo* |
| soup | zuppa | *dzooppah* |
| source | la sorgente | *lah sorjayntay* |
| south | il sud | *eel sood* |
| souvenir | il souvenir | *eel sooovayneer* |
| spaghetti | gli spaghetti | *lly spahgayttee* |
| spanner | la chiave fissa/la chiave per bulloni | *lah keeahvay feessah/lah keeahvay payr boollonee* |
| spare | di riserva | *dee reesayrvah* |
| spare parts | i pezzi di ricambio | *ee paytzee dee reekahmbeeo* |

| | | |
|---|---|---|
| spare wheell | ruota di scorta | *rwotah dee skortah* |
| speak (verb) | parlare | *pahrlahray* |
| special | straordinario | *strahordeenahreeo* |
| specialist | lo specialista | *lo spaychahleestah* |
| specialty | specialità | *spaycheeahleetah* |
| speed limit | il limite di velocità | *eel leemeetay dee vaylocheetah* |
| spell (verb) | dire come si scrive | *deeray komay see skreevay* |
| spicy | piccante | *peekkahntay* |
| splinter | scheggia | *skaydjeeah* |
| spoon, spoonful | cucchiaio | *kookkeeaheeo* |
| sport (play) | fare dello sport | *fahray dayllo sport* |
| sport | lo sport | *lo sport* |
| sports centre | centro sportivo | *chayntro sporteevo* |
| spot | posto/luogo | *posto/lwogo* |
| sprain (verb) | slogarsi | *slogahrsee* |
| spring | primavera | *preemahvayrah* |
| square | quadrato | *kwahdrahto* |
| square (town) | piazza | *peeahtzah* |
| square metre | metro quadro | *maytro kwahdro* |
| squash (to play) | giocare a squash | *jokahray ah sqoo-osh* |
| stadium | lo stadio | *lo stahdeeo* |
| stain | macchia | *mahkkeeah* |
| stain remover | lo smacchiatore | *lo smahkkeeahtoray* |
| stainless steel | acciaio inossidabile | *ahtcheeaheeo eenosseedahbeellay* |
| stairs | scala | *skahlah* |
| stalls | platea | *plahtayah* |
| stamp | francobollo | *frahnkobollo* |
| start (an engine) (verb) | accendersi/mettere in moto | *ahtchayndayrsee/ mayttayray een moto* |
| station | la stazione | *lah stahtzeeonay* |
| statue | statua | *stahtooah* |
| stay (in hotel) (verb) | essere alloggiato | *essayray ahllodjeeahto* |
| stay (verb) | rimanere | *reemahnayray* |
| stay | soggiorno | *sodjorno* |
| steal (verb) | rubare | *roobahray* |
| stench | puzzo | *pootzo* |
| sting (verb) | pungere | *poonjayray* |
| stitch (med ) (verb) | suturare | *sootoorahray* |
| stitch (verb) | cucire | *koocheeray* |
| stock, broth | brodo | *brodo* |
| stockings | le calze | *lay kahltzay* |
| stomach | lo stomaco/pancia | *lo stomahko/pahnchah* |
| stomach ache | il mal di stomaco/ pancia | *eel mahl dee stomahko/pahnchah* |
| stomach cramps | i crampi allo stomaco | *ee krahmpy ahllo stomahko* |
| stools | le feci | *lay faychee* |
| stop (bus/train) | fermata | *fayrmahtah* |
| stop (verb) | fermarsi | *fayrmahrsee* |
| stopover | lo scalo | *lo skahlo* |
| storm | tempesta | *taympaystah* |
| straight | liscio | *leesheeo* |
| straight ahead | sempre dritto | *saympray dreetto* |

| | | |
|---|---|---|
| straw | cannuccia | *kahnnootchah* |
| strawberries | le fragole | *lay frahgolay* |
| street | strada | *strahdah* |
| street side | lato della strada | *lahto dayllah strahdah* |
| strike | lo sciopero | *lo shopayro* |
| strong | forte | *fortay* |
| study (verb) | studiare | *stoodeeahray* |
| stuffing | ripieno | *reepeeayno* |
| subscriber's number | numero dell'abbonato | *noomayro dayllahbbonahto* |
| subtitled | con sottotitoli | *kon sottoteetolee* |
| succeed (verb) | riuscire | *reeoosheeray* |
| sugar | lo zucchero | *lo dzookkayro* |
| sugar lump | zolletta di zucchero | *dzolayttah dee dzookkayro* |
| suit | abito/completo | *ahbeeto/komplayto* |
| suitcase | valigia | *vahleedjah* |
| summer | estate (f) | *aystahtay* |
| summertime | ora legale | *orah laygahlay* |
| sun | il sole | *eel solay* |
| sun hat | cappello di paglia | *kahppayllo dee pahllyah* |
| sunbathe | prendere il sole | *prayndayray eel solay* |
| Sunday | domenica | *domayneekah* |
| sunglasses | gli occhiali da sole | *lly okkeeahlee dah solay* |
| sunset | tramonto | *trahmonto* |
| sunstroke | insolazione (f) | *eensolahtzeeonay* |
| suntan lotion | olio solare | *oleeo solahray* |
| supermarket | supermercato | *soopayrmayrkahto* |
| surcharge | supplemento | *soopplaymaynto* |
| surf (verb) | fare il surf | *fahray eel soorf* |
| surf board | tavola da surf | *tahvolah dah soorf* |
| surgery | ambulatorio | *ahmboolahtoreeo* |
| surname | il cognome | *eel koneeomay* |
| surprise | sorpresa | *sorprayzah* |
| swallow (verb) | inghiottire | *eengeeotteeray* |
| swamp | la palude | *lah pahlooday* |
| sweat | il sudore | *eel soodoray* |
| sweet | caramella | *kahrahmayllah* |
| sweet (adj) | dolce | *dolchay* |
| sweetcorn | granturco | *grahntoorko* |
| sweet dreams | sogni d'oro | *sonyee doro!* |
| sweeteners | la saccarina | *lah sahkkahreenah* |
| swim (verb) | nuotare/fare il bagno | *nwotahray/fahray eel bahneeo* |
| swimming pool | piscina | *peesheenah* |
| swimming trunks | lo slip/il costume da bagno | *lo sleep/eel kostoomay dah bahneeo* |
| swindle | truffa | *trooffah* |
| switch | interruttore (m) | *eentayrroottoray* |
| synagogue | sinagoga | *seenahgogah* |

## T

| | | |
|---|---|---|
| table | tavolino | *tahvoleeno* |
| table tennis | ping-pong | *peeng-pong* |
| tablet | compressa | *komprayssah* |
| take (verb) | prendere | *prayndayray* |
| take (time) (verb) | durare | *doorahray* |
| talcum powder | talco | *tahlko* |
| talk (verb) | parlare | *pahrlahray* |
| tall | alto | *ahlto* |
| tampons | i tamponi | *ee tahmpony* |
| tanned | abbronzato | *ahbbronzahto* |
| tap | rubinetto | *roobeenaytto* |
| tap water | acqua del rubinetto | *ahkwah dayl roobeenaytto* |
| taste (verb) | assaggiare | *ahssahdjeeahray* |
| tax free shop | negozio duty-free | *naygotzeeo dootee-free* |
| taxi | il taxi | *eel tahxee* |
| taxi stand | posteggio dei taxi | *postedjeeo day tahxee* |
| tea | il tè | *eel tay* |
| teapot | teiera | *tayeeayrah* |
| teaspoon | cucchiaino | *kookkeeaheeno* |
| teat | tettarella | *tayttahrayllah* |
| telegram | il telegramma | *eel taylaygrahmmah* |
| telephoto lens | teleobiettivo | *taylayobeeaytteevo* |
| television set | il televisore | *eel taylayveezoray* |
| telex | il telex | *eel taylayx* |
| temperature | temperatura | *taympayrahtoorah* |
| temporary filling | otturazione provvisoria | *ottoorahtzeeonay provveezoreeah* |
| tender | tenero | *taynayro* |
| tennis (to play) | giocare a tennis | *jokahray ah taynnees* |
| tennis ball | palla da tennis | *pahllah dah taynnees* |
| tennis court | campo da tennis | *kahmpo dah taynnees* |
| tennis racket | racchetta da tennis | *rahkkayttah dah taynnees* |
| tenpin bowling | bowling | *boleeng* |
| tent | tenda | *tayndah* |
| tent peg | picchetto | *peekkaytto* |
| terminal (bus/tram) | il capolinea | *eel kahpoleenayah* |
| terribly | terribilmente | *tayrreebeellmayntay* |
| thank (verb) | ringraziare | *reengrahtzeeahray* |
| thank you | grazie | *grahtzeeay* |
| thank you very much | mille grazie | *meellay grahtzeeay* |
| thaw (verb) | sgelare | *sjaylahray* |
| the day after tomorrow | dopodomani | *dopodomahny* |
| theatre | teatro | *tayahtro* |
| theft | furto | *foorto* |
| there | là | *lah* |
| thermal bath | le terme | *lay tayrmay* |
| thermometer | termometro | *tayrmomaytro* |
| thick | spesso | *spaysso* |
| thief | ladro | *lahdro* |
| thigh | coscia | *koshah* |
| thin | magro | *mahgro* |
| things | roba | *robah* |
| think (verb) | pensare | *paynsahray* |

| | | |
|---|---|---|
| third | terzo | *tayrtzo* |
| thirsty, to be | avere sete | *ahvayray saytay* |
| this afternoon | questo pomeriggio | *kwaysto pomayreedjo* |
| this evening | stasera | *stahsayrah* |
| this morning | stamattina | *stahmahtteenah* |
| thread | filo | *feello* |
| throat | gola | *golah* |
| throat lozenges | le pasticche per la gola | *lay pahsteekkay payr lah golah* |
| throw up (verb) | vomitare | *vomeetahray* |
| thunderstorm | il temporale | *eel taymporahlay* |
| Thursday | il giovedì | *eel jovaydee* |
| ticket | biglietto | *beellyetto* |
| tidy (verb) | mettere in ordine | *mayttayray een ordeenay* |
| tie | cravatta | *krahvahttah* |
| tights | la calzamaglia/il collant | *lah kahltzahmahlleeah/ eel kollahnt* |
| time | tempo | *taympo* |
| times | volte | *voltay* |
| timetable | orario | *orahreeo* |
| tin | lattina | *lahtteenah* |
| tip | mancia | *mahnchah* |
| tissues | i fazzoletti di carta | *ee fahtzolayttee dee kahrtah* |
| toast | il brindisi | *eel breendeezee* |
| toast (bread) | il pane tostato | *eel pahnay tostahto* |
| tobacco | tabacco | *tahbahkko* |
| toboggan | il toboga | *eel tobogah* |
| today | oggi | *odjee* |
| toe | dito (del piede) | *deeto (dayl peeayday)* |
| together | insieme | *eenseeaymay* |
| toilet | bagno/ gabinetto | *bahneeo/ gahbeenaytto* |
| toilet paper | carta igienica | *kahrtah eejayneekah* |
| toilet seat | sedile del water | *saydeellay dayl vahtayr* |
| toiletries | gli articoli da toletta | *lly ahrteekoly dah tolayttah* |
| tomato | pomodoro | *pomodoro* |
| tomato ketchup | il ketchup | *eel kaytchoop* |
| tomato purée | salsina di pomodoro | *sahlseenah dee pomodoro* |
| tomato sauce | sugo di pomodoro | *soogo dee pomodoro* |
| tomorrow | domani | *domahnee* |
| tongue | lingua | *leengwah* |
| tonic water | acqua tonica | *ahkwah toneekah* |
| tonight | stanotte | *stahnottay* |
| too much | troppo | *troppo* |
| tools | gli arnesi | *lly ahrnaysee* |
| tooth | il dente | *eel dayntay* |
| toothache | il mal di denti | *eel mahl dee dayntee* |
| toothbrush | lo spazzolino da denti | *lo spahtzoleeno dah dayntee* |
| toothpaste | dentifricio | *daynteefreecheeo* |
| toothpick | lo stuzzicadenti | *lo stootzeekahdayntee* |
| top up (verb) | riempire | *reeaympeeray* |
| total | totale | *totahlay* |
| tough | duro | *dooro* |

| | | |
|---|---|---|
| tour | giro della città | *jeero dayllah cheettah* |
| tour guide | accompagnatore (m) turistico | *ahkkompahneeahtoray tooreesteeko* |
| tourist class | la classe turistica | *lah klahssay tooreesteekah* |
| Tourist Information office | ufficio informazioni turistiche | *ooffeecho eenformahtzeeonee tooreesteekay* |
| tourist menu | il menù turistico | *eel maynoo tooreesteeko* |
| tow (verb) | trainare | *traheenahray* |
| tow cable | cavo di traino | *kahvo dee traheeno* |
| towel | asciugamano | *ahshoogahmahno* |
| tower | la torre | *lah torray* |
| town | città | *cheettah* |
| toys | i giocattoli | *ee jokahttolee* |
| traffic | traffico | *trahffeeko* |
| traffic light | semaforo | *saymahforo* |
| trailer tent | il carrello tenda | *eel kahrrayllo tayndah* |
| train | treno | *trayno* |
| train ticket | biglietto (del treno) | *beellyaytto (dayltrayno)* |
| train timetable | orario ferroviario | *orahreeo fayrroveeahreeo* |
| translate (verb) | tradurre | *trahdoorray* |
| travel (verb) | viaggiare | *veeahdjahray* |
| travel agent | agenzia viaggi | *ahjayntzeeah veeahdjee* |
| travel guide | guida turistica | *gweedah tooreesteekah* |
| traveller | il viaggiatore | *eel veeahdjahtoray* |
| traveller's cheque | assegno turistico | *ahssayneeo tooreesteeko* |
| treacle/syrup | melassa/lo sciroppo di melassa | *maylahssah/lo sheeroppo dee maylahssah* |
| treatment | trattamento | *trahttahmaynto* |
| triangle | triangolo | *treeahngolo* |
| trim (verb) | accorciare | *ahkkorchahray* |
| trip | gita/viaggio | *jeetah/veeahdjo* |
| trousers/shorts | i pantaloni (lunghi, corti) | *ee pahntahlony (loongee/kortee)* |
| trout | trota | *trotah* |
| trunk call | interurbana | *eentayroorbahnah* |
| trunk code | prefisso | *prayfeesso* |
| trustworthy | fidato | *feedahto* |
| try on (verb) | provare | *provahray* |
| tube | tubetto | *toobaytto* |
| Tuesday | il martedì | *eel mahrtaydee* |
| tumble drier | asciugatore | *ahshoogahtoray* |
| tuna | tonno | *tonno* |
| tunnel | galleria | *gahllayreeah* |
| turn | volta | *voltah* |
| TV | la TV | *lah TeeVoo* |
| tweezers | pinzetta | *peentzayttah* |
| tyre (bicycle) | il copertone | *eel kopayrtonay* |
| tyre pressure | la pressione delle gomme | *lah praysseeonay dayllay gommay* |

## U

| | | |
|---|---|---|
| ugly | brutto | *brootto* |
| umbrella | ombrello | *ombrayllo* |
| under | giù/sotto | *joo/sotto* |
| underground | il metrò | *eel maytro* |
| underground railway system | metropolitana | *maytropoleetahnah* |
| underground station | la stazione del metrò | *lah stahtzeeonay dayl maytro* |
| underpants | le mutande | *lay mootahnday* |
| understand (verb) | capire | *kahpeeray* |
| underwear | biancheria intima | *beeahnkayreeah eenteemah* |
| undress (verb) | spogliarsi | *spollyahrsi* |
| unemployed | disoccupato | *deesokkoopahto* |
| uneven | ineguale | *eenaygwahlay* |
| university | università | *ooneevayrseetah* |
| unleaded | senza piombo | *saynzah peeombo* |
| urgent | urgente | *oorjayntay* |
| urgently | d'urgenza | *doorjayntzah* |
| urine | orina | *oreenah* |
| use (verb) | usare | *oozahray* |
| usually | il più delle volte | *eel peeoo dayllay voltay* |

## V

| | | |
|---|---|---|
| vacate (verb) | lasciare libero/a | *lahshahray leebayro/ah* |
| vaccinate (verb) | vaccinare | *vahtcheenahray* |
| vagina | vagina | *vahjeenah* |
| vaginal infection | infezione vaginale (f) | *eenfetzeeonay vahjeenahlay* |
| valid | valido | *vahleedo* |
| valley | la valle | *lah vahllay* |
| valuable | prezioso | *praytzeeozo* |
| van | il furgone | *eel foorgonay* |
| vanilla | vaniglia | *vahneellyah* |
| vase | vaso | *vahzo* |
| vaseline | vaselina | *vahzayleenah* |
| veal | vitello | *veetayllo* |
| vegetable soup | il minestrone | *eel meenaystronay* |
| vegetables | verdura | *vayrdoorah* |
| vegetarian | vegetariano | *vayjaytahreeahno* |
| vein | vena | *vaynah* |
| vending machine | il distributore automatico | *eel deestreebootoray ahootomahteeko* |
| venereal disease | malattia venerea | *mahlahtteeah vaynayrayah* |
| via | per | *payr* |
| video recorder | il videoregistratore | *eel veedayorayjeestrah-toray* |
| video tape | videocassetta | *veedaeeokahssayttah* |
| view | il panorama | *eel pahnorahmah* |
| village | il paese | *eel pahaysay* |
| visa | visto | *veesto* |
| visit (verb) | visitare | *veezeetahray* |
| visit | visita | *veezeetah* |

| | | |
|---|---|---|
| vitamins, vitamin tablets | le vitamine | *lay veetahmeenay* |
| volcano | vulcano | *voolkahno* |
| volleyball | pallavolo | *pahllahvolo* |
| vomit (verb) | vomitare | *vomeetahray* |

## W

| | | |
|---|---|---|
| wait (verb) | aspettare | *ahspayttahray* |
| waiter | il cameriere | *eel kahmayreeayray* |
| waiting room | sala d'attesa | *sahlah dahttayzah* |
| waitress | cameriera | *kahmayreeayrah* |
| wake up (verb) | svegliare | *svayllyahray* |
| Wales | Galles | *Gahllays* |
| walk | passeggiata/ giro a piedi | *pahssaydjeeahtah/ jeero ah peeaydee* |
| walk (verb) | fare due passi | *fahray dooay pahssee* |
| wallet | il portafoglio | *eel portahfollyo* |
| wardrobe | guardaroba | *gwahrdahrobah* |
| warn (verb) | avvisare/chiamare | *ahvveezahray/ keeahmahray* |
| warning | avviso | *ahvveezo* |
| wash | lavare | *lahvahray* |
| washing-powder | detersivo | *daytayrseevo* |
| washing | bucato | *bookahto* |
| washing line | corda da bucato | *kordah dah bookahto* |
| washing machine | la lavatrice | *lah lahvahtreechay* |
| wasp | vespa | *vayspah* |
| water | acqua | *ahkwah* |
| water ski (verb) | fare lo sci nautico | *fahray lo shee nahooteeko* |
| waterfall | cascata | *kahskahtah* |
| waterproof | impermeabile (m) | *eempayrmayahbeellay* |
| wave-pool | piscina con movimento a onda marina | *peesheenah kon moveemaynto ah ondah mahreenah* |
| way | modo | *modo* |
| way (on the) | per strada | *payr strahdah* |
| way | la direzione | *lah deeraytzeeonay* |
| we | noi | *noee* |
| weak | debole | *daybolay* |
| weather | tempo | *taympo* |
| weather forecast | bollettino meteorologico | *bollaytteeno maytayorolodjeeko* |
| wedding | le nozze | *lay notzay* |
| Wednesday | il mercoledì | *eel mayrkolaydee* |
| week | settimana | *saytteemahnah* |
| weekend | il fine-settimana | *eel feenay saytteemahnah* |
| weekend duty | servizio di fine-settimana | *sayrveetzeeo dee feenay-saytteemahnah* |
| welcome | benvenuto | *baynvaynooto* |
| well | bene | *baynay* |
| west | ovest (m) | *ovayst* |
| wet/damp | umido | *oomeedo* |
| wetsuit | muta | *mootah* |
| what/how? | come? | *komay?* |

| | | |
|---|---|---|
| what? | che (cosa)? | *kay (kosah)?* |
| wheel | ruota | *rwotah* |
| wheelchair | sedia a rotelle | *saydeeah ah rotayllay* |
| when? | quando? | *kwahndo?* |
| where? | dove? | *dovay?* |
| which? | quale? | *kwahlay?* |
| whipped cream | panna montata | *pahnnah montahtah* |
| white | bianco | *beeahnko* |
| who? | chi? | *kee?* |
| wholemeal | integrale | *eentaygrahlay* |
| wholemeal bread | il pane integrale | *eel pahnay eentaygrahlay* |
| why? | perchè? | *payrkay?* |
| wide-angle lens | il grandangolare | *eel grahndahngolahray* |
| widow | vedova | *vaydovah* |
| widower | vedovo | *vaydovo* |
| wife | la moglie | *lah mollyay* |
| wind | vento | *vaynto* |
| windbreak | paravento | *pahrahveento* |
| windmill | mulino | *mooleeno* |
| window (car) | portiera | *porteeayrah* |
| window | finestrino/finestra | *feenaystreeno/ feenaystrah* |
| window pane | vetro | *vaytro* |
| windscreen wiper | tergicristallo | *tayrjeekreestahllo* |
| wine | vino | *veeno* |
| wine list | lista dei vini | *leestah dayee veeny* |
| winter | inverno | *eenvayrno* |
| witness | il/la testimone | *eel/lah taysteemonay* |
| woman | donna | *donnah* |
| wonderful | delizioso/bellissimo | *dayleetzeeozo/ baylleesseemo* |
| wood | legno | *layneeo* |
| wool | lana | *lahnah* |
| word | parola | *pahrolah* |
| work | lavoro | *lahvoro* |
| working day | giorno feriale | *jorno fayreeahlay* |
| worn | logoro | *logoro* |
| worried | preoccupato | *prayokkoopahto* |
| wound | ferita | *fayreetah* |
| wrap (verb) | incartare | *eenkahrtahray* |
| wrist | polso | *polso* |
| write (verb) | scrivere | *skreevayray* |
| write down (verb) | scrivere | *skreevayray* |
| writing pad (squared/lined) | blocco (a quadretti/a righe) | *blokko (ah kwahdrayttee/ah reegay)* |
| writing paper | carta da lettere | *kahrtah dah layttayray* |
| written | per iscritto | *payr eeskreetto* |
| wrong | sbagliato | *sbahllyahto* |

## Y

| | | |
|---|---|---|
| yacht | lo yacht | *lo eeot* |
| year | anno | *ahnno* |
| yellow | giallo | *jahllo* |
| yes | sì | *see* |

| | | |
|---|---|---|
| yes, please | volentieri | *volaynteeayree* |
| yesterday | ieri | *eeayree* |
| yoghurt | lo iogurt | *lo eeogoort* |
| you | Lei/tu | *layee/too* |
| you too | altrettanto | *ahltrayttahnto* |
| youth hostel | ostello della gioventù | *ostayllo dayllah jovayntoo* |

## Z

| | | |
|---|---|---|
| zip | la chiusura lampo | *lah keeoozoorah lahmpo* |
| zoo | lo zoo | *lo dzo* |

# Basic grammar

There are two genders in Italian, masculine (m) and feminine (f). This applies to nouns, articles (the/a) and adjectives.

## 1 Definite article

The form of the definite article (English '**the**') depends on the sound at the beginning of the word following it:

| | Singular | Plural |
|---|---|---|
| **m** | **il** bambino | I bambini (before a consonant) |
| **m** | **lo** zio/**lo** studente | **gli** zii/**gli** studenti (before z or s+consonant) |
| **m** | **l'**animale | **gli** animali (before a vowel) |
| **f** | **la** casa | **le** case (before a consonant) |
| **f** | **l'**amica | **le** amiche (before a vowel) |

## 2 Indefinite article

Depending on the sound of the following word, the indefinite article (English '**a**' or '**an**',) is:

| | | |
|---|---|---|
| m | **un** bambino/ **un** animale | (before a consonant or a vowel) |
| m | **uno** zio/**uno** studente | (before z or s+consonant) |
| f | **una** casa | (before a consonant) |
| f | **un'**amica | (before a vowel) |

The plural of the in definite article (English '**some**') are:

| | | |
|---|---|---|
| m | **dei** bambini | (before consonant) |
| m | **degli** zii/**degli** studenti | (before z or s+consonant) |
| f | **delle** bambine/ **delle** amiche | (before a consonant or a vowel) |

## 3 Nouns

In general:

Nouns ending in **-o** are masculine. To form the plural change **-o** to-**i**: (vin**o**-vin**i**)

Nouns ending in **-a** are feminine. To form the plural change **-a** to **-e**: (birr**a**- birr**e**)

Nouns ending in **-e** are either masculine or feminine. Learn each individually. To form the plural change **-e** to **-i**: il pied**e** **(m)** - **i** pied**i**; la nott**e** **(f)** - le nott**i**

Some nouns are irregular:
**la mano** (hand) is feminine
**il problema** (problem) is masculine

Nouns ending in **-ista** can be either masculine or feminine:
**il/la** dentista; **il/la** pianista

## 4 Adjectives

Adjectives tend to go after the noun they refer to. They must agree with the noun they accompany, both in gender (masculine/feminine) and in number (singular/plural).

| | Singular | Plural |
|---|---|---|
| **m** | **un ragazzo italiano** | **dei ragazzi italiani** |
| **m** | **uno studente italiano** | **degli studenti italiani** |
| **(m** | **un tavolo grande** | **dei tavoli grandi)** |
| **f** | **una ragazza italiana** | **delle ragazze italiane** |
| **f** | **una stanza grande** | **delle stanze grandi** |
| **(f** | **una stazione vicina** | **delle stazioni vicine)** |

## 5 Possessive adjectives

A possessive adjective agrees in gender and in number with the noun whch follows it, and not with the 'owner' as in English. It is usually preceded by the definite article:

| | masculine | | feminine | |
|---|---|---|---|---|
| | singular | plural | singular | plural |
| my, mine | **il mio** | **i miei** | **la mia** | **le mie** |
| your, yours | **il tuo** | **i tuoi** | **la tua** | **le tue** |
| his, her, hers, its | **il suo** | **i suoi** | **la sua** | **le sue** |
| our, ours | **il nostro** | **i nostri** | **la nostra** | **le nostre** |
| your, yours | **il vostro** | **i vostri** | **la vostra** | **le vostre** |
| their, theirs | **il loro** | **i loro** | **la loro** | **le loro** |

## 6 Personal pronouns

Since verb endings are normally sufficient to indicate who is doing the action, io, tu, lei, lui, etc. are only used for emphasis or to avoid confusion.

| | |
|---|---|
| I | **io** |
| you (singular and familiar) | **tu** |
| he | **lui** |
| she,you (formal) | **lei** |
| we | **noi** |
| voi (you, plural) | **voi** |
| they | **loro** |

## 7 Verbs

Regular verbs follow one of three patterns, depending on their endings in the infinitive.

| | **-are** | **-ere** | **-ire** |
|---|---|---|---|
| infinitive | **comprare** (to buy) | **prendere** (to take) | **dormire** (to sleep) |
| **(io)** | **compro** | **prendo** | **dormo** |
| **(tu)** | **compri** | **prendi** | **dormi** |
| **(lui/lei)** | **compra** | **prende** | **dorme** |
| **(noi)** | **compriamo** | **prendiamo** | **dormiamo** |
| **(voi)** | **comprate** | **prendete** | **dormite** |
| **(loro)** | **comprano** | **prendono** | **dormono** |